The Executive Blind Spot

How Misalignment with HR Impacts Your Bottom Line

By
YARA BANKS

The Executive Blindspot
How Misalignment with HR Impacts Your Bottomline

Printed in the United States of America

Paperback ISBN: 978-1-965319-15-4
eBook ISBN: 978-1-965319-12-3

Purpose Publishing

Purpose Publishing LLC.
13194 US Highway 301 South
Suite 417
Riverview, Florida 33578

www.PurposePublishing.com

Table of Contents

Introduction

Welcome! I'm Yara Banks, bringing 25 years of experience in human resources and business operations to help you explore how doing HR right can significantly impact your organization's revenue and profitability.

In my career, I've had the privilege of collaborating with diverse organizations, from innovative startups to Fortune 500 companies. One fundamental truth emerged from these experiences: the effectiveness of your HR strategy is intricately linked to your business outcomes. C-suite executives like you understand that success is not solely measured by numbers; it's also about harnessing the power of your most valuable asset—your people. As decision-makers, you face the pressing challenge of aligning human capital with your strategic objectives. This book serves as your blueprint for transforming HR into a key driver of business success.

We'll delve into essential topics, including how to attract and retain top talent, foster a high-performance culture, and implement leadership development initiatives that empower your teams. You will discover how effective HR practices can lead to reduced turnover, enhanced employee engagement, and, ultimately, improved financial performance.

But let's be clear: this is not about traditional HR practices. This is about rethinking your approach to human resources as a strategic partner in achieving your vision. When organizations prioritize people, they create environments that spark innovation, encourage collaboration, and drive growth.

As you read through these pages, I encourage you to challenge the conventional wisdom that HR is merely an administrative function. Instead, view it as a critical lever for organizational success. The insights, tools, and real-world case studies provided will equip you to make informed decisions that elevate your HR practices to the level of strategic imperative.

Thank you for joining me on this transformative journey. Together, let's unlock the true potential of HR to not only enhance your workplace, but also drive your organization's profitability and success.

Warm regards,
Yara Banks

Leadership Development

Missing Parts

As an HR expert that has worked with dozens of companies, ranging from high-watering earnings of eight figures and above, I've witnessed the internal structure of *countless* businesses. And in my close exposure, I've noted a lot of trends — both good and bad — that follow these businesses even as they grow.

You may scratch your head, but arguably, the most impactful duty in a company is often underscored. **Leadership development** is like the big step in an uneven staircase, one that, if missed, will topple you all the way down because of mismatched pace. Many big companies have this *go-go-go* mentality, and as a close source of mentorship for them, I have had to advise that to sustain success, pause and consider the building blocks you'll use to climb towards your goal.

To take that analogy a step further (pun unintended, but welcomed), a successful business' trajectory is upwards. That's why C-suite executives must take their business up the rungs at a careful rhythm — if you miss one beat, for example, the results can be catastrophic. Imagine climbing a stairwell where steps are missing. You may hop over a few gaps for a while, but stumble for even a quarter of a second and expect a sharp plummet down.

Once a company grows to a certain point, its market demand will call for leadership that is strong and focused. But a lot of C-suite executives traverse crooked stairwells. They inevitably stagger their employees by not paving a sensible pathway, and for their lack of planning, sabotage the progress that has been made.

In communication with HR, who promotes and hires professionals based on their value to the business, C-suite executives must emphasize protocols that teach the diverse aspects of leadership. As an HR professional who has seen this work well, I propose the concept of a "born leader" vs. "someone who's appointed to lead."

Born Leader vs. Appointed to Lead

Some people naturally possess leadership qualities. We're all aware of the humans who excel at certain skills — whether that be in sports or music — and grace them the title of talented, although we avert assigning those titles in the workplace.

Why, may you ask? At first glance, it appears unreasonable to claim that a certain skill is more favorable to certain personalities than others. I've observed that within a lot of workplaces, time employed, and a lack of glaring errors translates to company loyalty, which translates to obligated rewards.

And what greater award does HR offer but a shiny promotion?

This is where we broach a sticky dilemma: leaders who are born to inherit the task, as opposed to those who take it by circumstance. Often, the latter become delegates for a given project or passion not because of a thoroughly planned nomination, but because the situation asked for it.

Same goes for leaders who are chosen based on the seniority or team experience. So many companies endure cycles of steep highs and sharp lows — poor quarters, especially, can call for structure shakeups that propel those with longer experience to the top.

In times of uncertainty, it makes sense why C-suite professionals would default to experience over all else. Who wouldn't trust someone who knows the company policy like the back of their hand, who can count the steps from the entrance to the reception in their sleep, and knows every annual report since the start of the decade? There's value to be extracted from someone who doesn't need to be taught the company's ins and outs, when we're assuming they'll use that expertise to empower their team.

We can see the consequences that might call training's ROI into questions through this equation:

$$\textit{Training ROI} = \left(\frac{\textit{Net Benefits from Training}}{\textit{Total Training Costs}}\right) \times 100$$

Where Net Benefits from Training = Benefits from Improved Performance - Training Costs

If the percentage generated from this equation misses the 50% mark, then there is an evident loss from training new professionals.

The problem is that experiential advantages aren't that cut and dry. HR can recruit a new employee that shows promise and aptitude for their position within their first month, but because companies are so locked into the corporate tradition that "new = novice," they'll gloss over a qualified applicant for someone who brandishes more certifications. A C-suite's job is to produce positive results as efficiently as possible — if you're promoting unfit candidates to leadership roles without a holistic assessment of their equalities, you're going against that.

This information may be overwhelming, as it challenges perceptions that many businesses default to. Just look at some of the high-profile clients in my portfolio: I once was contracted to assist a near-2-billion-in-revenue international conglomerate. Prior to introducing my HR services, they struggled with a faltering reputation amongst stakeholders and diminishing workflow.

I brought extensive experience with addressing backlogs, and swiftly identified areas where this company could streamline its processes. For a business of that calibre, you'd imagine they'd have everything tightened and figured out, but their leadership direly needed coaching. That is where I came in to draw proposals that'd improve their efficiency, while molding teams that played to the company's strengths. Ultimately, the business responded positively to my procedures and have rebuilt their reputation. A rut that once appeared insurmountable was overcome with the help of my sharp input — and in this section, I'll touch on a few of the concepts that propelled this success story.

Job Proficiency Does Not Equal Leadership

Picture this scenario — you're communicating with HR to figure out which employees have been displaying the best performance in recent times. HR responds to you with a list of employees who excel at self-regulation and productivity in their given job. Let's say your brand's focus is retail — the "proficient" employees on the ground are the workers who complete sales, engage customers and show initiative in keeping the store in prime condition. The best supervisors on the ground are the ones who perform the best teams with achieving the aforementioned tasks.

...But the expectations drastically change when you get to the corporate standards of "proficiency." A cubicle worker might not need the same skills in interactivity and organization to be considered a good worker. They're beholden to completing tasks that generally require them to work independently.

On the flip side, the boots on the ground may be exposed to more customer interaction, but not necessarily have the tools to handle the backend components of a business. A qualified leader must be able to maneuver seamlessly between these two realms — understand what dynamics are influencing sales' success on the ground, while also being able to study the mechanisms that will shape strategies and marketing launches.

In case you're zoning out already, no, appointing the right leader isn't like trying to deconstruct the space-time continuum. I mean, it's clearly difficult to figure out what workers make a perfect fit, as I've had CEOs overseeing multi-million, sometimes even billion-dollar businesses gripe over this issue. But getting on top of this complexity only demands abandoning outdated rules and adopting more forward-thinking ways to assess employees.

For example, let's say that you're a C-suite executive overlooking a car sales company. You want to have new managers in your sales location and are looking at the employees with the least tardiness, lengthiest employment, and significant sales.

To no surprise, workers who have been under your company the longest crop up at the topic of the candidate pile. And they must be provided an ounce of consideration for how much background they have with the company, as the year and familiarity must lend an upper hand in higher-up positions.

But — because there is always a "but" — you may promote a more experienced employee and encounter a staggering issue. The same issues surrounding internal company culture plague the workers who have been with your company the longest. The workforce isn't a monolith, and not every single candidate will be the same, but when you broadly recognize people based on status rather than capability, who's to say that the person you promote will challenge the existing paradigm? And if they aren't producing innovative strategies that push their team every single day, then are they worth a leadership position in the first place?

This is all to say that a fresh pair of eyes can be a *positive* deciding factor. More than that, companies must remember to look at leaders from a holistic perspective — yes, an employee can be an absolute whiz at their responsibilities and merit recognition. But being a standout in a specific role does not necessarily mean they must be thrust into a position where they carry multiples more responsibility, on top of new skills to hone.

Inevitably, the higher you raise an employee in a company (particularly a big one), the more blind spots they will have to specific skills. For example, a person in marketing who works their way up the corporate ladder won't be able to speak for what goes on in the tech departments; at least, they won't be able to reference more than surface levels interactions with the team. To take it further, the longer someone spends in a position of elevated authority, the more probable it will become that they're removed from the day-to-day realities of junior positions.

You can analogize this phenomenon to a musician who makes it big. When they're starting out, they provide a USP that resonates with broad audiences for how relatable they are because they've been freshly launched from that audience. As time stretches on, their bond to that culture dwindles as they adopt a lifestyle that is far removed from their serviced demographic. It's like the saying, "to reach the top is the easiest part — staying is an entirely different challenge." And we picked at that saying prior in the book, but it is extremely relevant to what leaders endure when they're propelled from positions of less authority. So, you catch upper management's attention because you bring the boots-on-the-ground perspective they're missing — but can you hold onto that strength?

From my experience with ultra successful companies, a good leader will definitely answer "yes." Because a good leader isn't someone who "naturally" qualifies for authority because they hold expertise or intrinsic "ease" — they're someone who maintains the effort to stay attuned to boots-on-the-ground's weaknesses and strengths, tweaking their instruction based on what they observe from analysing various groups.

Leadership mustn't just be a dazzling prom crown that is placed upon those who show the most promise on a rigid checklist. It must be a continuous, *adaptive* assessment, one that considers a worker's proficiency in more areas than simply meeting their job's expectations.

Leader vs. Authority

Showing leadership and holding authority are two very different concepts. Sadly, they are often conflated by "powerful" supervisors and delegates who use their position as a shield, rather than its intended purpose — to guide a team.

"Power trip" is a phrase that's familiar to all of us. Even the prosperous companies I've worked with have regularly succumbed to this issue.

When a manager exploits their power to take advantage of employees, it's no surprise that the workers react poorly. Workplaces that don't regulate employer abuse often report high rates of turnover, sabotaged productivity, and a dip in professional reception. It is hard for employees to individually address these incidents because in the workplace, title is propped up above all else. If, for example, a sales assistant brings their own strategy from a previous job, their supervisor will be the ultimate judge on if they get to deviate from corporate standards. If everyone goes about their own routine, you end up with a company that lacks cohesion and vision. Simultaneously, you can't have a company that stifles workers to where they cower from taking any risks that'd forward the brand's growth.

As we discuss the drawbacks of improper leadership, you may be struck with a question — why do some leaders exploit their power? Not *all* managers go on power trips, obviously, otherwise no one would bargain their peace of mind with being subject to a corporate dictator (or, at least most people would opt out of that torture). The overarching commentary surrounding abusive managers is that they sabotage companies' growth because they refuse to absorb feedback and react healthily to change.

And that reveals the crux of the problem — undeveloped leaders exploit their titles, because they don't grasp how to properly use them.

To get a better idea, compare "authority brandishing" to "amateur experts." The latter describes those who speak on topics they have no, or poor knowledge of, on the basis they are qualified in some other field. And I'm not talking about stretching skills into adjacent disciplines — no, these people will have a PhD in astrophysics and also think they hold the utmost opinion on whether social studies courses are valuable! It's one thing for someone to relate their expertise to a relevant subject or inform themselves on a field they aren't quite familiar with to broaden their knowledge base; however, it is a whole other level of irresponsibility to assume that intelligence in one regard means that you carry expertise on every subject under the sun.

Here's a shocking revelation — everyone, including people in positions of power, has blind spots. Leaders stretch themselves as thin as possible so that they don't have any glaring gaps in their guidance, but it's impossible to be perfect at everything. That's why a faulty "authority" will waive their title to silence those who correct or challenge them, rather than face the reality of having to grow and improve every single day when you're looking after others.

Leaders aren't just people who have the privilege of dismissing and recommending workers — they establish credibility with those who respond to them, along with the audience that their company services, by modelling credible behaviour. Improper displays of authority only diminish a company's image from the inside out. Employees are much like pupils — when they're shown that petty methods are commonplace amongst those at the top, they'll model this uncivil behavior as it's their only frame of reference on the road to success.

Many authority figures think that they are above teaching the boots on the ground, that once they are elevated to a higher position, certain responsibilities are beneath them. But if anything, it's the opposite — you must be more concerned with leading by example once you're unable to directly or regularly oversee your team. It's impossible to be everywhere at once, and doubtlessly workers hold the individual responsibility to assure their own success, regardless of outlying factors. Considering this, a true leader must guide their team by emulating the behavior that helps a business thrive. If you're going to hassle an employee about how they treat company facilities, it'd be hypocritical to defy that principle when you're left alone with "superior" employees. The only lesson boots on the ground will learn is that so-called "poor" behaviour is acceptable to practice outside the awareness of disciplinary figures.

And trust me, the hardest workplace cultures to correct are those that are steeped in dishonesty. I've learned that billion-dollar companies can fix weak principles so long as the workers will adapt, but when they're accustomed to "fast-tracking" their way to success, you're left with a husk of a business, doomed to collapse. No matter how gargantuan a business empire may look, it can only endure if it self-regulates.

So, how can you avoid this catastrophic scenario where managers cannibalise the integrity of your business?

Be vigilant about appointing leaders who hold their position based on results, not title. Be receptive to feedback about performance aptitude, and when you promote workers, be clear about the expectations they're taking on with added responsibility. Leadership isn't merely a position you fill to strike off a checklist, nor is it a gap to be filled by any specialty, experienced candidate. It's a skillset that must be meticulously vetted, so you may promote with confidence.

Filling Seats, But Improper Qualifications

Speaking of being careful about who you elect to leadership, it's important that we address the fragility of leadership in general. Countless VPs have gloated to me, even after calling upon my counsel, about how they handle each job application like they're choosing the meal plan for a wedding after-party, and yet, the reality is that companies have limited resources to spend, and if HR mulled over thousands of candidates, they wouldn't be able to expend their skills efficiently.

You can calculate your own recruiting costs through this equation:

$$\text{Cost to Recruit} = \frac{\text{Total Recruiting Costs}}{\text{Total Number of Candidates Hired}}$$

Where **Total Recruiting Costs** Includes:

- Advertising Costs
- Recruiter Salaries & Commissions
- Job Fair Costs
- Background Checks
- Pre-employment Screening
- Software & Tools Used for Recruiting

We've already broached how leadership can emerge from circumstantial needs — when someone is thrust to the forefront of a cause because they happen to hold the most relevant expertise, or they're simply the first to take initiative. It's been established that while leaders can surface for reasons other than intentional appointment, "chance" doesn't often translate to appropriate skills. Even if someone has all the credentials to appear as a desirable professional on paper, it takes a lot more than skimming a padded resume to decide who's best fit to trust with your company's integrity.

And when it comes to dualling as an instructor and a role model, you can't slack on discernment.

To illustrate this point, let's touch on a weakness that emerges as companies grow; they get more resources, which you'd believe would produce more workers to strengthen their market impact. And this can be the case. Look at the most successful companies in the world, and you certainly see an enormous, complex workforce.

Similarly, you can look at some of the sharpest business downfalls in the world. Corporations have hired me to avert those outcomes, and I'll tell you that it manifests commonly as a phenomenon known as "too many cooks in the kitchen." I've talked to extremely successful VPs and C-suite professionals that'd completely dismiss this blind spot, believing that more talent in-house equates to higher returns.

In my professional experience, the correlation is rarely ever so linear.

The flipside to growing companies' potential is that bigger teams lead to increased blind spots. Using focus group meetings, I've studied that the upper management in many corporations can be skimmed (in both salary and number) by a ton when you consider their efficiency. This probably sounds wild, considering you'd expect multi-million-dollar companies to be the experts on optimizing roster efficiency. Nevertheless, you often discover in expensive bankruptcies and dissolutions that poor management isn't exclusive to smaller businesses. Many businesses skyrocket to success without addressing internal issues that hinder long-term growth.

Positions mustn't be filled for the sake of "getting rid" of gaps that have been identified by HR — yes, the accelerated nature of running a business doesn't allow for an exorbitant amount of time spent on the promotion/hiring process. Yet, the volatile nature of running a business is also cutthroat towards teams that don't manage themselves optimally, and that is a guaranteed effect of improper leadership. When it comes to appointing workers to positions of power, C-suite executives must communicate with HR, as well as involve themselves intimately, however possible, to ensure that major leadership positions aren't passed out to those who dazzle in credentials but not capabilities.

No Succession Plan for Transition

When a mountaineer is summiting a high peak, they brace for the altitude differences that will heavily impact their physical state. Matter of fact, years of research have shown that there are drops in oxygen that occur at different elevations on Earth. Those who inadequately prepare for these environmental changes can ultimately lose their summiting goal, just like workers who are promoted without preparation can plummet to failure.

Within companies, the consequences of improperly training workers aren't as personally catastrophic as improperly training to climb a high mountain — at least, when we're looking at sterile office spaces that are populated by corporate professionals. There are a lot of industries where poor training can produce immediate, fatal effects, but in the "backend" of a business, where you're exposed to more computers and paperwork than dangerous machinery, stressing protocol can appear frivolous. Especially when you view leaders from a self-sufficient perspective, it's easy to assume that they'd want to improve without external input.

Yet, like every other job, leaders depend on references to instruct their behavior. Just try to envision how disastrous it'd be if school boards took in teachers solely from passing the appropriate exams but showed nothing for binding course structures or teaching fundamentals. Schools would turn into the wild west. Lesson plans would vary widely depending on where you live, and many students would report unacceptable treatment based on no strict framework for their powerful leaders to adhere to.

Leaders also need guidance. People with power can bear the most influence on a company in both positive and negative ways. When companies aren't mindful about how they transition employees into powerful positions, they risk power abuse, or neglectful execution of authority.

It is also crucial that leaders aren't valued solely on how they please the gatekeepers — the authorities who "gift" them a privileged position. Leaders owe those they instruct to both push the bounds of the system and think critically for themselves to yield improvement. There's a regretful trend of employees climbing their way up the corporate rungs based on how they appease the needs of powerful authorities: running errands and taking unwanted tasks. While potentially indicative of a hardworking character, these aren't the only factors to consider when assessing leadership.

How do the leaders in your company serve the boots on the ground? Has there been a positive impact on productivity since their promotion, or a minimal if at all? I pose these questions to companies that I coach, extracting essential information across the hierarchy.

A leader's relationship to their team must take precedence above their perception amongst the company's most gilded members, who rarely interact with those who drive the business's day-to-day operations.

No Management Growth Track

Taking on a new position is like being inducted into a club. You can't stride into a community full of knitting fanatics, for example, and expect to get by with little knowledge of how a needle and thread works three months into your membership.

And that's a casual, optional form of engaging a passion. Compare that to a job, which you must certainly express interest for — in fact, you're paid to be passionate about improving your work, and still, this requires a direct reference for how success looks within the company. There's no reason that niche clubs boast more thoroughly constructed guides than powerful positions in a company. If someone partaking in an activity for free can grasp how a lack of knowledge will impact their contributions, then someone paid to perform at their best must be even more vigilantly instructed.

Many businesses believe that forcing employees through tutorials that repeat their mission statement — which can be accessed by anyone on the official website, anyways — *ad verbatim* suffices as informing them on the company culture. I'd say that's like directing someone to the FAQ when they ask a highly specific question. No matter how "advanced" an individual is in a company, they must be exposed to ways of informing themselves about the company values so that the culture remains cohesive and strong.

In addition, a lack of management growth track makes it harder for leaders to integrate into their roles. How can they evaluate their aptitude for employee engagement when they're hardly aware of what good performance looks like? An individual pathway, showing clear traits and milestones, can cultivate a desirable mindset. In practice, employees following this mindset will enhance manager-employee communication and emotional intelligence over time. A nonchalant attitude towards instruction of these aspects will result in leadership that lags behind, if not utterly fails.

Proactivity vs. Problem Resolution

Hectic workplaces. Pits of dread form in your stomach when you walk into a business that looks like it's in the heart of Armageddon. It's even worse if you work at this place, as you must clock into the chaos every single day and buoy through that.

Boots on the ground aren't the only ones who are adversely affected by a lack of management forethought, though it disastrously impacts morale and productivity. Leaders themselves will lose grip on their authority when they aren't taught to approach issues proactively, rather than retroactively.

This may sound contradictory, because our first association with problems is something that has already spiralled: an issue directly witnessed and is having a detrimental effect on structure.

We can compare this assumption to the leaky faucet that begins as a minor nuisance, but some weeks (if not months) down the line, the slight nuisance aggravates to an expensive problem that negatively impacts your regimen. An issue can crop up appearing minor, "negligible" if you justify not having the resources to address it at first; but as time passes on, it'll surely fester into a worse problem either by combining with other frustrations, or from the normal wear of leaving negative elements unattended.

Businesses with resource constraints can write off a negligible issue, if they deem to address it at all. These issues, while minor, can be deceptive. Managers that don't stifle blazes when they start as subtle flames will learn that they can quickly rage into infernos, and when the workplace catches fire, the fire will scathe anything adjacent, even if it had nothing to do with the fire's emergence.

So, an irresponsible manager will assume that it doesn't matter if a problem is swept under the rug so long as other parts of a team are in perfect condition. This mentality may lighten their current load of work, but ultimately, they'll be overwhelmed as they're "blindsided" by major issue after major issue, all seeming to pile up one after another. We've all heard of, if not personally endured, streaks of random bad luck. And in the waterfall of stress, it's easy to clam up and run away from the issues altogether. One problem is manageable enough in and of itself, but trying to juggle several resolutions, many of which are tied up in another inciting issue, is a gargantuan ask.

Leaders must be equipped to avert fires, not put them out. When a fire catches on, you can't predict if it will explode into an inferno or spark a countless array of blazes. A competent leader must mitigate hazardous behaviour that can fuel major backlash later on. It's much easier to address a problem in its infancy stages, both for the company's image and the employees' sanity.

Open Requisitions as Formalities

The issue of "gatekeeping" amongst upper management has become a popular topic in the workforce. Professionals fiercely withhold time from jobs with limited upward mobility, and from those where only an exclusive selection of people can access the most influential levels of the organization.

To combat the controversy, many businesses open requisitions as a formality. There are various other reasons upper management feigns to seek new leaders as well, such as pressure from internal politics. Existing leadership can cut corners, too, displaying the pretense of a recruitment process despite already deciding the outcome.

This highlights the issue of nepotism — promotions founded on the hands you shake rather than the moves you make. Connections are widely known to be an impactful factor on a worker's career success, and that's why networking events are such popular functions, as employees are encouraged to impress their bosses regardless of their job's runway.

Connections aren't always so bad when they're taken into career decisions. If you hear that a worker is reliable from an employer, it is understandable why you'd trust that peer's judgement while assessing the worker as a job applicant. We assess qualities other than academic credentials during the hiring process like character, so why wouldn't powerful references be considered the mark of a capable employee?

Well, that individualized aspect of connection is precisely why it can be so detrimental to company leadership. Experiences are specific to the employees that have interacted with each other, and not all personalities combine appropriately. Matter of fact, there is no objective stage to verify that these recommendations are factual results of a powerful work ethic — and not favors landing someone in a better position.

That shines a light on the insidious nature of nepotism. One can potentially, based on experiences that the general workforce is oblivious to and is unfairly barred from, gain favor with powerful leaders based on blood relation alone. The unrelated workers in a business can't vouch for whether this person has the skillset to capably lead them towards better productivity.

This all factors into a lack of healthy communication between various levels of a company. When upper management appears like this inaccessible, ivory-tower group that empowers through ambiguous ideals, then workers feel de-motivated, and that individual contributions have no meaningful impact. Employee morale is measured on the value their work seems to bring; if a high output is returned with poor labor treatment and a lengthy promotion process, then high turnover rates and toxic culture are all but assured.

$$Turnover\ Rate = \left(\frac{Number\ of\ Employees\ that\ Left}{Number\ of\ Employees\ at\ the\ start\ of\ fiscal\ year}\right) \times 100$$

Upper management can't reasonably communicate the justification behind every single decision, and that'd be an unnecessary burden on the employees they serve. What *is* crucial is to remember their obligation to the company is dependent upon the last point: serving their employees. A surplus of power does not nullify someone from workforce expectations, it broadens their responsibility (and compensation because of that). Internal politics are reflective of powerful authority that has lost sight of their responsibility to their team, and that marks a poor work culture overall.

Middle Management Must Not be Underscored

Thus far in this book, we've discussed the interplay between upper management and the by-line, and how the actions of both influence a company's success. Analysing both extremes helps paint a picture of how different positions of individual power shape a company's impact. Boots on the ground tend to mobilize in numbers, meaning that it isn't enough for sprinklings of workers to gather efficiently — a team is valued based on their overall output, therefore will be assessed as a collective.

$$Productivity = \frac{Total\ Output}{Total\ Input}$$

Managers, however, don't get to blend their performance with their peers. They are essentially competing with their peers or predecessors to be seen as the most competent leader. And that drives a lot of responsibility to these individuals — which, for C-suite executives, is reciprocated with uncontested authority. This level of autonomy is sadly not afforded to the authority who make many decisions but don't reside at such a high level, otherwise known as middle management.

Middle Management are the amphibians of a business. They can morph into both the team players and the team leaders, depending on what the situation calls for. In some instances, they're the medium between upper management's directions and the boots on the ground's execution of those instructions. They act as direct witnesses to what unfolds on the frontier and are obliged to ensure that the workplace models company expectations.

Middle management is the chief complaint in businesses, and it is absolutely *not* their fault.

For workers who are so involved in translating the company's mission to so many members, middle management often runs into "bottleneck" constraints where they are not prepared nor empowered to make changes. Their authority isn't as emphasized and vouched for. They may shy away from making tough calls that will influence specific issues because they do not believe they hold the power to shift the paradigm. This is reflective of how middle management is recognized within the company culture, whether that be in the form of reception from those they oversee or being backed up by upper management.

No leader should feel reluctant to bring positive change. Middle management is present to perform the duties upper management can't, but if their responsibility is treated passively, then a company can swiftly fall into disorder. It is essential, through thoughtful confidence, that even lower levels of authority are taught to exercise their positions. When middle management does not take the initiative to shift issues within the company culture, they risk binding the upper and lower levels into a freeze. There's no proper connection between the two, and neither appears to absorb the feedback necessary to thrive and advance as a company.

Opportunities

We've gone through the complexities of healthy leadership within a company, the factors that can produce unfavorable expressions of authority, and why certain environments and traditions cultivate the issues. The information can be overwhelming, as we all know change doesn't happen overnight. If your business has been inadvertently contributing to the faults emphasized prior, it will require constant, labored dedication to uproot these weaknesses and turn them into positive improvement.

Talking of improvement, the concept can be a vague, head-scratching puzzle. It's one thing to identify that your business has weaknesses in its culture that need to change. It's especially easy for an outside perspective to burst in and proclaim what faults need to be corrected, while those who've been steeped in a habit for so long will struggle to realize how their behavior reflects under a different lens.

You'll want to employ specific strategies to yield specific changes — changes that positively shape the leadership in your business. But where to begin when the problematic methodology has become culturally ingrained?

To start, build a comprehensive management roadmap. This outline can be the yellow brick road to follow with end goals in mind. Next, promote from within, onboarding the employees that you see as long-term investments, hoisting them to more influential positions. As mentioned earlier, loyalty and experience don't necessarily serve as qualifications for greater responsibility. At the same time, barring the general workforce from career mobility will produce other unwanted effects: nepotism, political promotions, interference in decisions that must be limited to merit.

From the hiring process to the training stage, employees must be clearly informed how to heighten their involvement. HR, for example, must craft onboarding sessions where they can present solutions to general interview questions like, "where do you see yourself in five years?" Both job candidates and supervisors must have a clear conception of what a successful career trajectory looks like in your business.

Present Pathways with Endpoints

As opposed to inquiring about an employee's personal career outlook, present tracks with solutions to gauge how long they plan to stay. Ultimately, it is impossible and unrealistic to expect every professional to stick with your company for the long term. Even Ivy League universities, which the whole nation of America fight into, never claim zero dropout rates. If the most prized institutions in America fail to retain all their membership, then there's no reason to find fault in your company for experiencing the same.

Businesses must prepare to lose employees and extract resources to polish workers who will ultimately take their skills elsewhere. It can be bitter to watch a highly trained employee scout the market for a position elsewhere, a position that didn't contribute nearly half the resource to priming them for the job. But a worthy investment isn't necessary converting workers into infinite resources — even if someone is equipped to perform optimally during their temporary employment, they'll be a net positive to the company compared to an influx of directionless workers, inconsistent with their goals, and lacking concrete vision for their company role.

Not to mention, having a positive impression on workers yields employees who'll recommend you positively elsewhere. Businesses themselves benefit from cultivating environments that are attractive to ambitious professionals. Word of mouth spreads like wildfire in the digital age, and the days of NDAs binding criticism of internal operations are no longer. Aspire to draw the top crop of potentials, and thereby raise the bar for adjacent businesses to do the same. That way, you'll have a stronger selection of candidates to sift through when hiring time comes.

Succession Planning

Succession planning is the crux of strategic management and leadership development. It maintains order in an organization and its core vision, even through inevitable changes in workforce.

Proper succession planning is not only an initiative-taking tactic to avoid poor leadership choices, but it also aligns the business's human capital with its financial goals, thus producing a smooth transition in leadership roles.

To make the fullest use of succession planning, we first must grasp on what it entails. Succession planning is the process of choosing, then developing employees to fill key leadership roles. You'd prep workers to step into higher positions as they become available, ensuring that the organization can function effectively without interruption.

As organizations are dynamic in nature, succession planning must adapt to these changes. It's not a static process. Rather, it evolves alongside the organization's growth and shifting needs.

From onboarding, workers must qualify themselves for higher roles. It mustn't be a matter of "applications are posted, everyone scrambles to present their performance as attractively as possible" —that'll only foster a culture where productivity is tied to immediate rewards.

Think about how restaurants receive their safety certifications. Every food-handling business understands that inspectors can drop in at any time to validate the quality of their service, although they'll be informed beforehand that they're due for a check-in. This "covert" method of evaluating businesses assures customers that when they walk into a restaurant, they aren't being subject to service that is below the tier of standards set by accredited agencies. You don't stumble in on the day of inspection and notice that all the surfaces are polished, the floor is swept, and the food is safely prepared, then arrive the next to see that the establishment has descended into total neglect. While we can talk about how important it is to practice integrity in all facets in life — whether it be in the workplace and outside of it — the reality is that people will cut corners where they see that they can reap more value out of doing so. Thus, if you don't normalize a culture where self-regulation is mandated every single day, then people will take it as a cue to slack off until a visible assessment is in place.

Be like the governmental inspectors when it comes to vetting your leadership. Employees must be encouraged to display their personal initiative over an extended period — not just when they've racked up a certain number of years and thus are considered having met the "bar" for a greater promotion.

How, may you ask, can you motivate a new employee to perform like they're being currently assessed for a promotion? That's a challenge that can only be addressed by acknowledging outstanding performance reports. Give recognition to the employees who show quick or phenomenal improvement. Inform employees that extraordinary output will lead to increased opportunities in the future. What many businesses get right is that they highlight career opportunities in the onboarding process — but a failure to reinforce that, as employees get integrated into the workplace, can make promotions seem like a nebulous, inaccessible goal.

There's a belief that some people learn best through visual learning, while others are drawn towards the more tactile. You could say that exposing workers to the recognition of their peers (by recognizing those at different levels of an organization, not just the most powerful) is a way of providing physical evidence that consistency is valued in a company. Remember that boots on the ground are a lot like pupils, especially before they're morphed into leaders — they absorb the culture surrounding them like sponges, so if a lack of transparency and accessibility is what they're subject to in the formative stages, they're less likely to form a loyalty to the organization. Without loyal workers who emulate company values, you can't shape leaders for the next generation.

Tie People to Dollars, and Dollars to Your Boots on the Ground

By this point in the book, you've probably realized an overarching theme that defines many of our lessons — and that is increasing efficiency by recognizing the monetary value of workers.

C-suite executives hold ultimate authority over many levels of an organization. With so much power, it can be stifling to figure out how to optimize strategies for the better of all teams involved. While it's important we don't reduce complex, unique issues into single resolutions, a steadfast approach can be tying people to dollars, and dollars to your boots on the ground.

You see, many setbacks that confront businesses are related to inefficient resource management. Not taking advantage of opportunities that'd elevate the brand's position in the long term, due to short-sighted decisions, generally fall into the following categories:

<u>Habit</u>

Company culture is the cornerstone of a successful business. If you want to succeed in a competitive market, you must market a vision that stands out amongst competitors — and what better way than with a strong vision?

Like actual political factions, companies champion their own internal values so that they present a uniform brand to the public. As we've broached in earlier sections, this can present a helpful reference for employees to meet when they join the team. But all practices must be done in moderation, and

C-suite executives must be mindful of how their standards grow to the ever-changing demands of modern times.

If Walt Disney stuck to the same 2D, made-for-cinema format past its 100-year reign, it'd never become the multi-billion dollar conglomerate it is today. Us as consumers can clearly identify the core values of its brand: family-friendly content above all, and a franchise centring princes and princesses that champion moral themes. On the surface, Disney sacrificed certain traits that made its brand so distinctive in earlier times. You can find animations that emulate the same style as Disney's top motion artists, and I'd bet the company is constantly studying the graphics of animated competitors to meet their techniques.

This isn't a sign that they're diluting their vision. They're adapting to the shifting demands of audiences, who are seeking increasingly realistic content to relate to. Compare the astronomical gross of Rapunzel, a 3D princess film, that was released in the same timeframe as Princess & the Frog, one of Disney's last major 2D princess launches. Princess franchises have always been the company's biggest cash cow; the budgeting of both aforementioned films proves no different. The companies' choice to advance with one franchise, however, and embrace tradition with the other, leads to staggeringly contrasting outcomes. Had they put all their investments into the 2D film, they wouldn't have seen positive returns during that period. Even the biggest global corporation was forced to adapt to avoid a very expensive lesson, and with how dynamic the digital age has made success stories, brands are just as interchangeable as employees.

No one must believe they're above evolving.

<u>Poor Management</u>

Ultimately, if a company goes through a period of stagnation, the driving force to mitigate this should be leadership. C-suite executives have a greater scope of how business decisions impact the profits their company gets from each project and product launch. While the boots on the ground collectively contribute to the overall execution of a brand's vision, C-suite executives call the shots on when a strategy must be recalled or reshaped. It is crucial that they understand their responsibility.

How Do These Gaps Impact Dollars?

When you encounter failure in your personal life, it's hard to not feel dispirited. You may have spent a long time working towards a goal, and even if the ambition was never more than castles in the air, you assigned a level of purpose to one day achieving it.

It's hard enough failing independently. The stakes raise to an entirely new level when you have others dependent on your success, and you still produce dismal results. Then it's not just you who suffers from the fallout — multiple others will be affected. This can create a ripple effect, where tangential causes suffer as well, and if the outcome is catastrophic enough, your ambition may collapse altogether.

Businesses are a lot like extended group projects. Each member is a component in completing the assignments, and the assignments align one after another as steps towards reaching completion.

You can't isolate building leadership in a successful company. Rather, consider it a wheel that helps churn the 24-hour clock. If the machinery isn't working, the bell won't chime. And even if you've set up the parts to function correctly, maintenance must be attended to keep that condition.

You're probably thinking, what's so big about a clock not working, though? Most people reference their phones for the time. If the analog clock isn't working in the office reception, it's not like the employees can't go to some other resource to see the time, right?

Absolutely, there are almost always alternatives to keep operations buoyant in times of crisis. A successful business will have "backup" services to maintain the flow when the standard offerings don't go as intended.

But consider some place like London, where Big Ben striking the time is integral to the culture. If it suddenly went down for months, that'd surely have an impact on the country.

And although we might question if anyone is visiting an office to view a clock wind its hands around, standard components not being in working order can produce long-term problems. It may start as negligible as the analog clock being neglected because the manager decides it's not worth fixing. But then that lackadaisical attitude trickles into other issues, and you see bigger consequences that hurt the morale and productivity of the team.

Employees are highly reactive to the balance of their workplace — the conditions of the facilities, internal dynamics, and leadership will influence how they interact with the business. When you fail to retain hires based on poor management decisions, you'll have employment to be paid and burn heaps of money on recruitment processes that don't bear any long-term positives.

The hiring process is extensive and burns HR resources. While it's regular to seek out new candidates as a business reaches significant milestones, and to replace the natural in-and-out cycle of professionals in the corporate world, companies mustn't splurge considerable budget on the hiring process. Beyond setting up interviews and marketing your job postings on multiple platforms, the labor doesn't stop when you've got an employee on your team. Afterwards, there's a period where they'll extract more resources from your company in the learning process that is onboarding and accustoming themselves to business protocols. If the organization doesn't have a clear set of values or way of vetting workers, then you'll wind up with a "dead load" of employees that heighten salary costs but don't produce the best output.

Not to mention, countries like America are entrenched in their litigious era. It is no exaggeration to say that lawsuits can be whipped out of the most minor offenses nowadays — and this isn't to trivialize the very extreme cases of negligence that can occur in workplaces, but rather to inform those who run businesses that they have much to lose as authoritative entities.

Companies Do Not Budget for Bad Management

Companies do not incorporate the costs of poor management into their budget. Generally speaking, a business will divest their resources into analysing the net positive effects to occur from successes, while mitigating the chances of failure if any step fails along the way.

The problem with this lies in the fact that it depends on all factors being isolated from outside influence. You can, for example, pass an improvement plan onto middle management so that they can coach boots on the ground — but if they don't explain that instruction rightly to the intended audience, every step afterwards will be in jeopardy. It isn't just consumer reception that companies need to account for when poor leadership is at play. They also are forced to clean up the faults of costly lawsuits, sabotaged product launches and a possibly damaged reputation amongst the public.

These days, the pervasiveness of social media allows for both customers and workers to provide immediate feedback on a business. And once a controversy spirals — which, given the engagement-fuelling algorithms of social media, is incited for the sake of reaping profits for tech companies — a company's PR can get out of control. No amount of press releases penned by your media relations team or attempts by HR to reach out to disenchanted employees can fix a media windstorm that will ultimately stain your brand for as long as the results appear on Google. You can't completely wipe controversies now that the web platforms individual creators, many of which will be everyday customers who witness the organization of your business. If they encounter signs of poor management, the current culture won't be forgiving of your mistakes.

So, remember to foster a company culture that doesn't factor in cultural failings as expenses as you would taxes and salaries. A business's motive is to produce the most profits through the most efficient methods in the end, and poor management is only counterintuitive to that.

Look to Online Communities for Communication Techniques

It's no secret that many businesses have chosen to "shun" social media, only catching onto its value as more influencers and independent personalities proved its lucrativeness. Email marketing campaigns are largely a strategy of the past — you'll still see businesses sign you up for their mailing lists, but the best method of reaching people is through social media when you want to sell.

But what if I told you the same could be applied to the internal framework of businesses?

You see, the end-customer interaction is shaped by planning behind the scenes. Social media marketing is a tool that is cultivated by teams that can consist of dozens, professionals that study the online trends of users and convert that into effective marketing tactics.

Social media posts aren't just a great way of connecting with popular opinions. They can be used to inform and shape company processes. Just consider the immediate feedback cycle of modern celebrities, whose social media comment sections can influence the presentation and collaborations of their brand. They get instant feedback on each move they publicize with their world, and in turn, carve their image to one that is more favorable to yielding monetary support.

Businesses must do the same when they're mapping conversations between HR and C-suite. More than ever before, it is so easy to access the insights of people at different levels of an organization due to the transparency social media allows. Anyone can get onto a forum and feel empowered to share their personal experiences — sentiments that can inform a business's internal practices for the better. You don't have to endure negative feedback when you work proactively to avoid the incidents disenchanted workers report.

Fiduciary Responsibility: Managing People as Assets

In a business, it'd be short-sighted to account for only physical assets — cash, facilities — as investments to look after. You must be vigilant about the team you foster as well. Your team's efficiency will ultimately drive the success of your business.

That's why it's so important that the highest authorities in a business absorb feedback that will grow effective leadership.

A problem businesses encounter is that their asset portfolio in terms of employees (paying unemployment, time off) isn't being tightened or verified. This can produce severe, avoidable losses.

Responsibility to Stakeholders and IPO, People Who Buy Stock

Investors in your company's success expect that you optimize operations to produce the most returns. You can't prioritize cultural comforts — internal company politics, favoritism, and so on — when others' money is on the line. It isn't just the reception of customers that you'll sour with poor leadership, it's the people who inject funds into your business that help it grow.

Ultimately, C-Suite executives can avert this issue by grasping that their choices don't impact those in immediate sight. Nor must they seek validation for those who are in their immediate cohort alone. A smart C-suite executive, who genuinely desires to ensure the health of their business, must seek feedback from people at different levels of the organization. There's a reason large corporations consider shareholder opinions whenever they make business decisions. And that isn't to say that money must take precedence over sensibility — shareholders, too, are vulnerable to stagnation and may shun change because they've put money on the line. You can't depend too heavily on any single perspective because they have their own risks that your decisions impact.

Ultimately, effective leadership development boils down to practicing discernment. This is a skill that is built over intentional, consistent dedication to learning and teaching others.

When employees can look to authority who are genuinely invested in their improvement, the worst consequences of toxic work culture can be avoided. C-suite executives are obligated to be aware of the need of those that they serve, and that comes from having transparent dialogue and expectations. When you individualize these lessons for your own business, you must find noticeable improvements in productivity as authority ingrains these principles.

KEY TAKEAWAYS

Leadership development is a multi-pronged, multi-step process. Take it from the words of a HR professional who has counseled dozens of C-suite executives — you'll need positive training strategies in order to yield the results you desire, especially when it comes to leadership. Habits inspire long-term change, and habits don't just fall from trees; you must pause and assess how your current approach is affecting the self-sufficiency of your employees.

Recruiting & Retaining Talent

Areas of Disconnect, the Opportunities, and Stories/Experiences

Employees are the backbone of any successful company — this is no secret to the average worker, who must reconcile this every time their employer holds any "productivity" check-in. My career involves exploring a lot of businesses' frameworks; while actively immersing myself in various company cultures, I've observed meetings centered around scrutinising dips in performance. I understood that these were major stressors for those in the upper management suite, but when I talked to the boots on the ground, this approach showed no differently than an uptick in grumpy murmurs from their leaders. Frankly, it's hard to connect people who stand so far from each other in terms of day-to-day responsibilities on corporate values. A sales assistant for a retail brand, for example, might be more concerned with customer interactions than the consequences of shrinkage, which trickles upwards to workers, who, despite being less immediately involved in the issue, are more invested in mitigating its occurrence.

If you're a C-suite executive, you've probably spent a lot of time considering how the makeup of your company impacts quarterly reports. Businesses flourish when they are on an upward trajectory — when your staff are about as motivated about the company mission as they are about replacing the filter that has been left to mold in the coffee machine for weeks, underperformance is only expected. You want to cultivate a robust foundation out of your workforce, which is achieved by hiring the right people.

...which leads us to the often resented, envied, and underappreciated, HR.

Recruiting, interviewing, and searching for talent sounds like a relatively manageable (no pun intended) burden to muster, if just for the fact HR's expectations aren't as broadly described as other employment titles. Raise your hand if you've ever gone job hunting to find that the "entry-level" position you stumbled across entailed saving babies in housefires and delivering fresh coffee to your leaders before sunbreak. Advertised at the standard pay of a standard job in your field, of course, because those cunning HR recruiters must be getting compensated for squeezing you for every drop of labor you're worth.

In truth, HR has to account for a lot of responsibilities — you could argue, even, that their focus is a lot broader than the average job.

Yep — you read that right. Those "overpaid" professionals are ensuring you have a lot more returns than they're being paid for.

Before you skeptics reach for your tinfoil hats, consider this question — what is the universal mark of a competent employee? A strong work ethic? A collaborative personality? A padded resume?

Think about this for a second or take a glance at the number of employee screening processes that go wrong — horribly wrong, because the corporate hiring machine is dependent on a bunch of attributes that can be easily faked. Everything from the social media trails HR investigates, to the glimmering CV that paints a promising picture of the candidate being assessed, is vulnerable to fabrication. It's not like someone is going to present an unflattering image of themselves when they are competing against other, sometimes dozens upon *dozens* of other, qualified talents who've scoured long and far for your job opportunity.

At the end of the day, where there is competition, there will be exploitation. And while we don't like to tread into paranoid territory, you don't need a tinfoil hat to grasp that the job market, as saturated as it is, attracts a lot of people who will take every measure to secure success.

Thus, begging the question — how does HR find appropriate candidates for the job?

It's easy for C-level executives to point their fingers down from their ivory towers, but hiring isn't as seamless a process as one might assume. HR professionals must grapple with the shortcomings of standard screening methods, particularly the ease at which people can "buff" their qualifications.

REAL LIFE CONNECTION — TECH TROUBLES

When a New York startup launched their marketing campaign, they were confronted with a swift setback. Writing, trivial as it may appear in today's job market, is a crucial skill that connects your business with wide audiences. Turns out the average New Yorker isn't all that enchanted by tech lingo, spoken almost exclusively by the STEM elitists who think that anyone who isn't pursuing a coding degree is determined to be poor (or deserves to be, anyways).

The tech startup was confident that their product would resonate with people once it got in their hands. Regardless, it's hard to sell people on an idea, especially when that idea rubs them like a cactus in the Vegas desert. Persuasive writing is the art of convincing people that they could forfeit logic for emotions, a tactic the startup desperately needed if they wanted to avoid a product that's dead upon arrival.

They tried fun little promotional games and dug into the depths of their skills for a get-out-from-jail-free card. But if there is one thing that holds true for business, it's that costly problems require costly solutions. You don't reap a million dollars off a penny unless you've hit it big in the lottery (and even then, lottery tickets sell for more than a cent nowadays, this isn't the 70s or *Willy Wonka*). Likewise, you won't sway people's perceptions without hiring an expert who knows how to spin compelling narratives.

With heavy hearts and (thankfully) heavier pockets, the startup's C-suite executives resigned to hiring a technical writer. Not your Shakespeare-fluent/Hemingway skin-walker type of English graduate, but a writer who could build the company's reputation while championing the qualities of its existing workforce. *Partially* because adding another one of "them" would make the ego blow of the marketing campaign a tad less painful; *mostly* because they'd rather not spend the extra time correcting someone who'd confuse MacBooks for netbooks in an article.

Henrik, the company's CEO, proudly put his recruiter to search for their ideal candidate. They were told to model the job posting based on similar positions for writers. No point in wasting more time crafting a totally new advertisement, Henrik reasoned, and so the totally-not-replica-of-The-Washington-Post-job-posting was published.

Responses came quickly. Writing degrees were in demand, so there was no shortage of talent to sift through. All of them claimed to have a penchant for STEM articles, as they did for all topics because they were writers. The HR professionals didn't think to question this because they were not instructed to judge based on the technological projects in their resume — rather, they assessed standard factors, like their alma mater's prestige, ability to access past references, and a clean digital presence. They trimmed the candidate pool down to a few dozen people and called them in for interviews.

Note that at this point, the tech startup had dedicated hundreds of dollars to recruiting and screening this batch. When you consider the HR professionals' clocked hours, and the productive output disrupted by a lack of talent, the startup was actively losing money the longer they didn't find the right hire. Hence, you might imagine that Henrik and his peers began pressuring HR to expedite the process. Their job started when HR produced returns that could be assessed. HR's responsibility, on the other hand, relied on expectations that were distributed hastily and haughtily. You can predict how this would breed disastrous results.

The startups' attractive tech salaries attracted a crop of Ivy grads — a selection of the best talents America had to offer. Yet, the "technical" writer they took in, Marie, didn't know a lick about tech. She boasted of her acclaim in academic circles, but that didn't extend to an industry she never broached. Because the startup neglected emphasizing the specialty they wanted to tap into, they wasted money on a hire who knew about as much as the existing staff on how to capture buyers. Which, considering the failure of their previous marketing campaign, wasn't saying much.

Now, this miscommunication between HR and C-suite wouldn't be so bad if Marie was determined to learn on the job. She'd still be stacked with a tall hill to climb compared to someone who met all the qualifications, but she could gradually fill in the company's weaknesses. However, Marie was resistant to taking extra learning on the job. She believed that her higher academic background made it insensible that she, given all her laurels, must attract any criticism of her capabilities. It didn't help that Henrik wasn't a stellar communicator. Feedback that should've been impartial was delivered with Marie at fault, rather than the faulty job posting that mis-identified her shortcomings in the first place.

KEY TAKEAWAYS

Degrees don't always amount to success. This information might be hard to process given that both C-Suite executives and the HR professionals they oversee are expected to have some academic certification, whether that be an MBA or studying Administration. Society in general teaches us that more education equates to more competency, and who would entrust themselves to a scalpel-wielding surgeon who credits their knowledge to binging all seasons of *Greys' Anatomy*. (Considering how long the series has gone on, that is a testament to diligence itself, which is an important trait when you're responsible for several-hour operations. Nevertheless, not the sort of experience you can qualify in an assessment)? There are certain fields where degrees strongly measure someone's professional capability, while for others, it may just be a fancy sticker.

See it this way. When scientists perform experiments, what is the disclaimer they attach to each finding? Okay, the only research you're familiar with is the anecdotes fed through your social media feed, but for those of you who don't know, case studies must account for one crucial factor: labs observe phenomena under *perfect conditions.* We're talking about a sterile environment where every effect is produced exactly how it is supposed to.

In the real world, you can't prevent random chance, you can't stop outside elements from interfering with results. Someone can flaunt a fancy degree from the best institution in the country, but you don't know what they did to get there or how that reflects on their personal ethics. Although colleges ideally admit students who show the most tenacity out of all candidates, people are admitted for different reasons, and someone might succeed in written tests despite not studying at all. They might not care to put much effort into what they do because they have succeeded in getting by with the least amount of effort possible, which would cause problems in a collaborative environment like a workplace.

When you assess employees from a *holistic* perspective, you'll realize degrees aren't necessary to most entry-level positions. In fact, they often exclude people who possess the positive character traits that translate to a strong, consistent work output which are the type of employee any company could only dream of having!

But wait, if you're one of said degree holders, don't chuck your ribbon diploma in the bin just yet! The paper certification isn't totally useless, since most companies persist in using this as a metric to hire employees.

Whether you're a fresh-faced hire whose eyes are set on becoming the next Jeff Bezos or are already in the position of a C-Suite executive and are looking to breathe a burst of productivity into your roster, it helps to know the fundamental traits of a good employee. Reliability, listening skills, and a constant drive to outperform oneself sound like traits on a profile from dating app heaven, but they're also the gist of someone you'd want to have as your staff. What good is it, after all, to have an Ivy League grad who clocks in every blue moon and thinks that their way is more sensible than the people they're managed by? Of course, if you can get someone who combines the ideal traits with a prestigious academic background, then you might as well pat yourself on the back for finding your golden goose. But if you're dealt the luck of the bulk of us and aren't a ticket away from winning the jackpot, then you'll likely encounter a situation where you'll have to draw a line between the two. *What matters more for an entry level hire: a degree or the right traits?* And when that time comes, the integrity of your company's operations depends on prioritizing what upholds its values.

Now that we're ending this chapter, you might be shaking your head in bafflement at the hiring criteria you've used so far, or you might be basking in pride for already having assembled the solution yourself. It's okay, we all learn and grow — and if you look at statistics, you'll realize you're not alone if this is a new lesson. Out of a pool of 80 requisitions (this is pulling from a job analysis that has been performed and analysed in real-time), 72 required that candidates have a degree. Imagine that! Just 10% of employers emphasized qualities outside of a piece of paper. We can lend the benefit of the doubt and assume those were all technical specialties, or we can consider that only three employees said that a new hire would need a degree to do their job. Clearly, we have a lot of work to do to reform our culture's perceptions of competency.

Secrets to Disrupting the Status Quo (Making Opportunities)

Have you ever looked at a company's accounting book and felt your eyes nearly bulge out of your skull from how slim the margins are? Even if you've never watched an episode of *Shark Tank*, as a C-suite executive, you must know a business' health is determined by how much it profits. It means little if you produce a revenue in the millions yet take home just under a thousand — rather, the realization might be crushing as you tuck the thin wads of cash into your staff's hands.

So, how does that relate to optimizing your workforce? As a professional in charge of managing several employees, it is important that you make decisions that ensure the longevity of their employer, and consequently, their job. A business that is set to fold in a couple of weeks is obviously not an attractive prospect, especially if you aim to hire the best talents. Your priority must always be keeping an eye on margins through revenue highs and lows as the percentage you profit will determine if your business is sustainable.

Which is a lot more achievable when your workforce isn't eating a huge amount of your operation costs.

Doubtlessly, finding the right balance for employee salaries is always a challenge. How do you tell the Harvard grad that their $400,000 in education will only earn them a quarter back, if not less, in their first year in the workforce? Rising costs of living have made the best crop of workers more selective of which positions they choose. As you might imagine, that translates to higher wage expectations.

But salary isn't the only measure of a quality job, just like an Ivy background isn't the sole measure of a competent employee. You must seek to compel candidates in ways other than direct financial compensation. If your company offers essential products, for example, you can bundle that into their benefits at a reduced cost. Healthcare, Dental, and other insurance can be supplied in bulk at a greater discount compared to if they were provided individually. There are many methods to be economic with employee compensation, even if standards have become much higher in recent times.

That isn't to say that every candidate will immediately buckle to your offer. Any candidate who is aware of the current job landscape and knows how to advocate their talents will demand a salary that is not just in line with industry standards but surpasses it. You may ask, why would an entry job embolden someone to think they must be paid like a senior employee? If you're not a tech recruiter who has seen some salaries thrown by computer science graduates, this will probably raise an eyebrow, but it's a general truth that people don't like to feel as if they're being cheated. And with nepotism and elitism still running amok, workers are inclined to shoot above their budget to ensure they aren't being undercut in favor of someone else, particularly someone who is less deserving.

Understandably, your knee-jerk reaction might be to insist that you are, in fact, fair with your hiring practices, and have never roped someone into a lowly paying job while expecting 10 years of loyalty before dreaming of fair compensation. Nevertheless, numerous people have observed the inequities levelled against previous generations in the workforce and would rather not make the same mistakes. It is your responsibility to establish a middle ground between satisfying the candidates that best fulfill your roles and understanding where an expense goes from beneficial to detrimental. They say that a good investment is priceless, but if a dozen Ivy grads cause your business to go under, then you'd have been just as well recruiting from the local gas station. Either way, your company would head to the same place; you'd just have less money left over for yourself through the downfall.

REAL LIFE CONNECTION — INDIE MEDIA COMPANY

Two women who have been best friends for life start a YouTube Channel. They start off small, uploading skits in their downtime between 9-5 jobs and the regular demands of adult life. They quickly gain traction on the platform for how relatable their content is: fuzzy home videos that remind viewers of themselves, and eventually end up making millions.

At this point, they quit their job and turn video making into a full-time endeavor. Weekly uploads turn into daily, and the women's frequent interactions with fans fuels a parasocial demand that shoots them to greater financial heights. They're guaranteed ten times the income of a day job by just switching on a camera, and the only bar to their increased success is time. They're a two-woman team, and determine they'll need additional help to churn out more content, reaping more dollars as a result.

They get to recruiting online. As a two-women business, it is only natural that they lack the hiring resources of a traditional company. There is no HR to guide them to the right talents, scope out which talents would be the best fit for their company, or counsel them on what their budget will allow.

It isn't as if the women couldn't hire an HR professional at this point. They could hand over the responsibilities to someone more qualified and continue with their video productions until their team fills out. But ego gets in the way of reason, and the women decide that since they were able to reach unfathomable fame and success on their own, they must be able to whisk through unrelated fields as well.

You probably don't need to imagine how this goes incredibly wrong.

They hire based on what responsibilities they'd like to get quickly delegated to others: video editing, filming, even a personal assistant to run errands whenever they get hungry or need a second cup of coffee. The list of needs is never-ending for the two business owners, but they justify it on the basis that they've averted support for so long and are only picking from the best crop of talent. Another glaring mistake, they've yet to realize, but they hire expensive graduates from the best schools to feel that they're paying extremely qualified employees. And these employees might *be* very qualified, given that they don't know how much their salaries are cutting into the business's margins. The owners project that with increased output, they'll be able to cover and even surpass the costs of additional wages.

This estimate ends up being brutally incorrect.

As it turns out, what brought the two video makers to fame — personability and relatable comedy — diminishes as they add more people to their team. The precision and glamor of Harvard creatives clashes with their unrefined brand, which unintentionally embraces the messiness from operating on a basic foundation.

The poor audience reception could've been avoided by taking a different route with how they directed their team. Had the women instructed their new hires to push concepts that aligned with their existing brand, they wouldn't have encountered the negative reception that came with expanding their team. But like the impending financial difficulties, this is ultimately the fault of two hopeful entrepreneurs betting on more than they could vouch for. The women failed to take on new talents based on a conservative analysis of past profits, instead going on the optimistic outlook that they'd be producing exponential revenue with additions to their team.

While having more people to produce content allows the women to create more revenue opportunities from their fans, the lack of success of their recent pivot sabotages the plans they had in mind. Ultimately, they've dug themselves into a deep hole where they need to simultaneously figure out how they can recapture disillusioned viewers *on top of* solving the pay issue that burns a bigger and bigger hole into their budget.

KEY TAKEAWAYS

As touched upon earlier, shinier doesn't equate to better. Someone can strut into your interview room with the best college in the country printed on their resume, but it is possible that they aren't the best fit for your company's current situation. Cost-per-hire is a very important component of managing a healthy business; the more your employment costs cut into your profits, the more likely it is you'll run into difficulties if an unfavorable financial quarter/quarters arrives.

Note this *Cost per Hire* equation as your business undergoes hiring cycles:

$$Cost\ per\ Hire = \frac{Total\ Recruiting\ Costs}{Number\ of\ HIres}$$

Perhaps this is an ambitious assumption, but I doubt you have ever heard of a business that has survived a terrible financial season despite their thin margins. Margins are everything, whether you're seeing record-high revenue or drowning in the lows. You must keep account of that percentage, and as a sacrifice, be conservative of which candidates you allow into your pay pool.

Oftentimes, it is best to keep a rusty ship afloat than to send a golden canoe out to sea. One is sure to flounder and considering it will go under before it meets any other signs of civilization, it is not as if it will attract recognition for its efforts. If anything, the creator's reputation will be tarnished because they missed constructing a practical product for their mission. Meanwhile, a rusty boat may not entice the pickiest of customers to get onboard, but it will achieve its purpose and satisfy a chunk of customers as a result. The profits gained from that success can fund future ventures, and hopefully allow for you to upgrade to more expensive pursuits in the future.

In essence, before you jump to climbing Mount Everest, make sure that you can summit the basic hills. Don't rush to hire the fanciest, priciest of talents simply because they will give you brownie points amongst the corporate ilk when you haven't built up the foundation to support them. The slow and steady win the race in the end.

COMMUNICATION

Have you ever walked into a business and thought, "Who in the world runs this place?"

In case you haven't caught on, I don't mean this in the wondrous awe sort of way, the fasciation you get when you stumble upon a hole-in-the-wall gem that must be getting more than a couple of customers per hour, but instead remains a secret to just you and the stream of loyal customers.

No, we're posing this question to shed light on a disorganized business. The companies that miss basic practices that'll help them reach efficiency, to the point that you question if there is even anyone in charge. The answer is obvious; there is at least one or two people behind the wheel — that is who ensures everyone and the lease gets paid (unless they're some money-laundering front meant to drive away people on purpose, but we'll assume the businesses in your side of town aren't out of some Hollywood thriller), and as far as they're concerned, fewer customers means less opportunity to achieve that goal.

Then why do some businesses look like they're straight out of a zoo? We're not just talking about family mom-and-pops that can wave away criticism on the excuse that they're just starting out, although people *will* flock to wherever the best service lies in the end. We're speaking about C-suite executives of eight or nine-figure companies — sometimes, even higher figures — that fail to get a hold of the most basic tasks. Their accounting is not in order. No one appears to be reachable when you dial their Google-provided contact information (you note that it hasn't been updated in the last decade). Everything about the business seems set up to fail, and you're left scratching your head as to why someone with so much money on the line could let things spiral to such disaster.

Communication drives the issue.

As a C-suite executive, it's easy to assume from your salary and status that you're exclusive from the other staff — that you can hole up in your office and never have to think about the other workers outside of your bubble because that is not what your role entails. While it might not be explicitly outlined on paper, someone in your position heavily depends on being in tune with the average worker's thoughts: their perceptions, their work qualities, how they're performing daily. And you can have someone hand off a report detailing all these observations to you at the end of the day, certainly, but there is one sphere where you really don't want to risk misinterpretations: talent recruitment.

C-suite goals must be understood by hiring reps. If you're looking to fill a gap in customer engagement with boots on the ground, requiring candidates who exemplify personability and communicative skills, your interviewing process won't fare well if HR sends out a generic advertisement for people who meet basic job qualifications. You need to emphasize what is needed on the team, and work with HR to verify that these qualities are being scouted out amongst the available workforces. It does nothing for your company if you hire more of the same issue. In fact, you just dig yourself deeper into a money hole because you'll waste time and company resources on employees who would've never met the standards in the first place. When it comes to skill sets, be firm and be clear. HR cannot read your minds, although it'd be fantastic to have employees who intuitively understand your every grievance.

DIVERSITY

Many people recoil at the mention of diversity. Their thoughts spring to sanitized workshops organized by faceless management, or pamphlets that reiterate the golden rules of empathy that you've recited since elementary school.

Our current landscape — politically, environmentally, professionally — is a lot better than the previous when it comes to recognizing inequality. At least, most people would see the immediate issue in putting up a job advertisement that is exclusive to a privileged majority. There are many hiring practices that you can't get away with in contemporary times due to decades of revolutions and law reformations, but that does not mean the corporate world is perfect yet in its demographic makeup. Minorities are less likely to hold higher-up positions. They are vastly overrepresented amongst boots on the ground, but climbing up to roles of magnified respect and responsibility remains a challenge. DEI initiatives are a partially mandated response to these flaws, enforced by government officials who believe that it is the only way to get companies to address leadership issues.

Sadly, anyone who has spent a significant amount of time in a workplace would know that these initiatives often don't stretch beyond surface level. Maybe you will get a presentation on the racist roots of America and a little exercise to challenge preconceptions on minorities, but there is rarely ever a follow-up to rearranging the physical makeup of companies. Realistically, institutions propped up on the mission of multiplying profits don't care to concern themselves with endeavors that don't help that goal. If a progressive campaign doesn't contribute to positive media coverage, thereby increasing goodwill towards their products, what is the need to partake in it? Staff rearrangements are quiet and yield subtle results; the public won't be instantly privy to the shakeup until the results affect the services or products they purchase, and as a C-suite executive, your mind won't instantly consider diversity as a way of optimizing output.

Not realizing that your view is incredibly outdated.

When you look at the studies, molding a diverse workforce reaps positive results for a company's performance. Talents get to enjoy widened access to opportunities they wouldn't normally reach because of superficial factors, and under-qualified candidates are filtered out as irrelevant advantages aren't factored in anymore. Think of it like this: when you're recruiting candidates, who do you want on your team? The daughter of the technology supervisor who has attended the best state school but barely shows any creativity or unique skills, or the applicant who graduated from a middle-of-the-road college, but is noted for their strides in extracurricular competitions and performing reputable research while they were still in school.

I think I'd go with the latter.

Diversity doesn't mean "forcing" underqualified workers into roles they don't deserve or have the skillset for. Diversity emphasizes a holistic mindset, which means challenging your preconceptions on who deserves a better training process and opportunities to enrich their output. It isn't fair to write one employee off for having less managerial experience when the other has only ever shadowed at their parent's company, where they likely were subject to less scrutiny and dubiously even performed in a fair environment. Invest in the talents you take on regardless of their background, because the choice to let certain people lag behind will only affect your company's success in the end.

Think of this saying: "if you fish in the same pond, you will get the same fish." You can never expect to produce anything new, creatively, or financially, if you stick to the same mechanisms of decades past. Sure, you could counter with the adage that "what's broken doesn't need to be fixed," but in today's dynamic market, everything goes out of season *fast*. The old practices that captured insurmountable success are swiftly replaced by new ideas that spring day by day in the digital era, because we're competing with so many people for a shrinking pool of consumers. With consumer discernment at an all-time high, companies can't afford to skip their strongest approaches to capture the market. Diversity is a necessity, not an optional add-on to squeeze out more profit.

$$Diversity\ Hiring\ Rate = \left(\frac{Number\ of\ Diverse\ Hires}{Total\ Number\ of\ Hires}\right) \times 100$$

Your company onboarding starts the moment the first requisition is posted. Just as you've learned to optimize communication with HR, adapt to strengthening the relations between other staff and C-suite executives. New hires must be informed on all the ins and outs of the organization — not just shoved into a repurposed storage room to complete an onboarding tutorial. You want to make your resources welcoming and effective. Where multiple companies fail is providing resources that are either weak in the engagement department or shove too much into too little of a timeframe to absorb the breadth of information.

Put yourself in the shoes of your candidates. Yes, you hope to select from the best of the best available, but not even the smartest humans can claim supersonic memory. Give new hires ample room to adjust to your company's culture so that they integrate into the environment with the correct mindset. It is better to reach the desired result at a prolonged pace than to headrush into a lagoon with no conception of how you missed the opposing shore. An employee who at least understands where they fall short and needs to improve is better than one who is hopelessly dependent because they weren't equipped with the right tools to thrive under your expectations.

Disconnects with Retaining Talents

Ever tried online dating? According to statistics, most adults have, and for those who haven't, you've likely heard the horror stories of dating app meetups gone wrong. Being put face-to-face with someone who completely deviates from your expectations is a jarring experience. What do you mean luscious-headed Joseph with a passion for baseball in fact sports a spotless scalp, and is only connected to the Little League through the signed (fraud) baseball they pawned off some shop in third grade?

It is only natural that humans react adversely to disappointments. When you come up short as a consequence of your own weaknesses, you recognize what you've done wrong and can set up an action plan to improve for future scenarios. But when someone else sets you up for failure? It is frustrating, on top of repelling.

That is a huge problem with company courtship practices. A lot of C-suite executives struggle with devising onboarding practices that introduce new hires to the same culture they were promised in interviews. Overselling is a fault attributed to both the talents and employers in today's landscape because people keep being showered with promises that can't be kept.

The hiring process doesn't end when the interview door is shut. Onboarding is perhaps the most important part of the recruitment process. You've found your golden pick, plucked them from their usual space of comfort, and plan to play on their existing skillset to the benefit of both your company and their personal growth. Productivity is maximised when employees feel like they're guided to success, that their individual performance ultimately amounts to more than a number in a sea of competing talents. You want to remind your employees that their input matters not just when you choose to hammer them over the head on company policies during droning meetings, but by nurturing them as they integrate into your company.

Additionally, you want to champion company loyalty by rewarding leadership for competency, as opposed to fulfilling the metrics for tenure. Many C-suite executives fall into the trap of shaping their company structure based on the standard "book" for corporate optimization: seniority seen as more experience which is seen as more qualifications, while fresher faces are counted out of managerial positions because no one wants to risk putting them above entry roles too early in the game.

In reality, ageism is a significant problem in modern workplaces, but seniority politics plays a huge part in it. Promoting people based on the amount of time they've spent with a company incentivise people to seek growth after a certain point. What reason is there to try to improve, after all, if they'll be awarded with the same compensation and recognition after they reach a certain point? Especially if peers that have been in a company for the same amount of time witness someone assume a leadership role just because they were the lottery pick in their "hiring group." They will assume their opportunity has passed by and see no reason to stand out.

Be vigilant and be connective. Employees must see they are part of a greater ecosystem that relies on their productivity, and the people occupying the top of the hierarchy aren't just ivory-tower cynics who dispose and pluck people based on superficial metrics. We want to destroy the notion that "career development is not about the grades you make but the hands you shake." In other words, supporting the unhealthy culture that interpersonal privileges must matter more than professional competency.

Now, don't misinterpret this. How well employees get along with their colleagues, particularly their leaders, matters a lot in assessing their capabilities for leadership. No one wants to work under someone who is surly with criticism and curdles at collaborating with their fellow professionals. Recognize those who thrive in a team setting and can solve problems on their own but beware of the promotions that sprout from nepotism or favoritism. "Seeing the potential" in the employee who brings the hot coffee to your desk every morning is obviously not a trait to consider in one's work assessment, let alone if they share your surname. Sadly, these advantages influence many company structures and lead to people leading others when they desperately need to be led to competent performance themselves.

Retaining Talent Opportunities

Remember report card season when you were younger? Wondering how in the world slacking on your project with procrastinator Maria and infamous delinquent Tom equated to "poor leadership qualities?"

We all grow and realize how much the success of a team depends not on just its individual components, but its holistic competence. We need leaders because it is far too often when you put a bunch of smart minds together, and they flounder to reach a reasonable middle ground. What happens when you encounter a group with strong headed personalities? Nobody agrees, no one wants to think someone else may be right in each scenario, and whoever is deemed to "win the argument" will take ownership of the consequent grade.

That isn't to touch on the multiple scenarios where outspoken people drown out the more timid. Drawing out the opinions of others from the sidelines is a tough challenge, especially when you aren't equipped with the skills to read emotions. That's why strong leaders are the bedrocks of successful companies.

Businesses are collaborative exercises. No matter if you're running with one staff and contracting your work to outside personnel or are a C-suite executive responsible for the performance of thousands of people, you must know how to look after a team and cultivate success strategies.

Leadership development is a crucial step in ensuring the success of new hires. They're the fish-out-of-water when they enter your company, no matter how hard they may try to put up a know-it-all front. With the diverse array of personalities that comprise the workforce, it is inevitable that you'll pluck from a variety of personalities — some less forward, some more prone to taking initiative when they need help, and some learning at lightning speed while others wind up becoming the instructors of evolved methods once they learn your methodology.

It's no secret that C-suite executives love to rush the onboarding process because they can't immediately correlate the success of their company to the training they utilize. Corporate culture is all about streamlining, which to the layperson manifests a lot like rushing through processes that require a lot of time to get done right. If you want to produce quick, cheap results that may only show their faults in the long run. Indeed, expediting the hiring process can look like an effective strategy, but it is no long-term solution. To maximize the productivity of a new batch of hires, you want to assign a mentor who possesses a lot more company insights than they would, understands how to pass down their knowledge in a way that is inviting and comprehensible (basically, when HR receives complaints that your favorite to-the-point manager is in fact a big bully who chides people over showing up with undone laces, then take their comments seriously), and knows how to grasp diverse groups of people.

Sadly, the last point is severely lacking in a lot of modern workforces. Too often, companies find themselves stretched thin from controversies arising from higher-ups who clearly have no idea how to interact with people from diverse backgrounds. Take the publicized instances of Black women being reprimanded based on their cultural hairstyles, for example; if your staff don't understand how to differentiate between box braids and a "messy appearance," then they need to be instructed behind the scenes before they make anyone else feel uncomfortable for their background.

Also, this returns us to our point on inclusive promoting practices. Do your higher-ups have a bias towards men, particularly White straight men? I know this might rile familiar emotions of feeling lectured by DEI representatives, but to enrich your company and the community you serve (assuming that you believe your product adds value to society — if not, then small expectations must be set for your business), you need to evolve with the times. Yes, that involves catching up on centuries' worth of ideals that've unfairly placed certain groups above others, idolized some for their contributions while others were belittled or blatantly stolen from.

You wouldn't like to work for someone who turned a blind eye if someone claimed your work as their own, would you? You also wouldn't be a fan of a manager who clearly favored the work of people who had a certain appearance. Being surrounded by professionals that reflect a singular complexion or expression of style can be daunting for those who don't fit neatly into society's categories. It's imperative that you shape a workplace that is welcoming to all backgrounds and has accessible resources and spaces for all identities.

GROWTH PROGRAMS

Remember the point earlier about avoiding boring onboarding tutorials? Almost every company opts for the cheap, basic practice of putting their employees in front of a screen, where they won't have to pay anyone to spend their time training someone else, until the new hires answer enough questions right to be brought out of the trenches. It's a pretty outdated and dreadful practice, if you can imagine reading all hundred pages of Microsoft Word's User Manual — even computer users in the 90s would rather pull up a VHS tape.

Extending beneficial offerings isn't just about having resources available for your employees, it's about compelling them, encouraging them to reach for greater heights as they join your workforce.

Low on ideas? Think about creating a targeted program. Factoring in the company culture you seek to create, prepare pamphlets, exercises, community-building opportunities that encourage employees to integrate into a certain outlook. After all, you can't throw a youngling defenseless into the wild and expect them to learn how to hunt. Everyone learns differently, but to account for everyone's preferences and weaknesses, you want to have hands-on instruction in tandem with verbal and written variations. By understanding the standards they are expected to meet, they won't have room to wriggle out of reproval must they ever deviate from standards. This especially holds true for the more unsavory of professionals. Unfortunately, there are a lot of individuals in the workforce today who cling onto sleazy ideas of how they must treat other people. They infringe on others' personal space, most commonly women, and sling inappropriate jokes that were "fine with John when he was supervising their shift." You want to avoid enabling those employees. For the average person, basic rules around consent are easy to understand so long as you're capable of compassion and listening. But not everyone functions from a respectful upbringing, and for the wellbeing of your employees, you must audit the "bad apples" who bend every rule they figure can be overlooked.

Employees need to be aware of the career growth opportunities you have at your company. It might seem like a frivolous task considering all your company positions would be publicly available; job posting and increased laws around transparency of company's internal practices has allowed that, but when employees gauge that you are not motivated to inform them of what strides they can make in the future, why must they do the grind in the present? From their point of view, your lack of interest in coaching them, molding them into future leaders, is a sign that someone else is being prepped for the position. Or the position is not within reach at all. Too many workers can attest to sour experiences of overwork by "ancient overlords," in professional terms: higher-ups who have clung to their roles for so long it is hard to recall a time they haven't been bossing people around. Understandably, when you have someone who knows the company's in-and-outs and has remained loyal for a long period, you want to retain them. But companies don't revolve around one individual — not the CEO, not the worker who bags the goods, not the HR who takes on the newest batch of workers. A company's success relies on the holistic efficiency of many, smaller parts. The employees, the strategies, and the business practices all contribute to producing increased success each quarter. When you fall short on one factor, you'll notice subsequent shortcomings in the other. Narrowing in your focus on a singular component is a setup for failure.

If your company has long survived on old ideals, then it may present a tough challenge to deviate now. You'll have to communicate with HR to sift through a well of feedback and remarks that will ultimately help you improve company leadership. Remember, a business' success is consequential of holism, thus you can't sweep away your problems forever. Affiliate your employees with leaders who promise a hopeful outlook for the company, and vet your existing workforce to check that they embody characters that agree well with looking after others.

YOUR TALK BETTER MATCH THE WALK

Ever watch a runway show? In this instance, it's probably best not to quote the episodes of *America's Next Top Model* considering the leadership exemplified on that show is anything but what we'd encourage for a corporate environment. But a broken clock is right once a day, and there is one saying that holds true in both the fashion world and business: your talk better match the walk.

It's easy to stomp around your company telling others how to improve, where they fall short and where they must grow their strengths, because you're not the one in charge of making that progress. Frankly, many bitter relationships between C-suite executives and HR professionals are not just from miscommunication over hiring practices, but people who hold less power within companies feeling like they are burdened with responsibilities whipped up by someone who has no scope of what their day-to-day work entails.

If you were to draw another industry parallel, it is like when a celebrity goes from rags to riches, building a career off relatable music that resonates with the working class only to get whisked off to a glitzier lifestyle. Suddenly, the compositions about starting from nothing become a little too generic and offensive — when was the last time they worked the same jobs you do, the last time they even stepped on public transit? Of course, you can always inform yourself about different lifestyles through research that don't involve you living them directly, but there is a stark difference between recognition and understanding.

C-suite executives must be mindful that their day-to-day responsibilities represent a completely different reality than the people they manage, and that can obviously fester negative assumptions from the latter. No, you don't need to do a workplace tour every day of the boots on the ground; you don't need to hassle the HR team about looking through their files or help write up a job posting for Indeed. Another gripe non-C-suite executives tend to have with upper management is feeling like they are over-supervised, barred from the freedom of acting upon their job as they'd like. Let your employees take full accountability of their roles, but don't hesitate to explore their realities and feedback from time to time to ensure that you set expectations from a place of reason. Imagine being asked to cook a dozen pancakes while your boss has only supplied you enough flour to bake six — those sorts of mix-ups you don't want to burden your employees with.

Walking the talk also relates to embodying your company mission. You, as a C-suite executive, are the closest representative to a "Face" of the company. Your identity might not be plastered across sponsorships or advertised to the public, but when employees see your name signing off a new policy change, it is important that you aren't caught doing the exact opposite of that standard during your time at work. For example, it is unrealistic to demand copious amounts of output from your HR team when it is known that you have been reducing hours for upper management since you've been in charge. Times can get tough in a company, and sometimes certain positions need to pull their weight, but just because some employees are failing doesn't give others the prerogative to go on victory runs and ignore the struggles of their colleagues.

Be a helping hand. By sending the message that you are open to providing resources that will aid your employees in enhancing their performance for future assessments, they'll see that they work for a company that cares about their employees' successes and doesn't view them as disposable pieces to be discarded and switched out at a moment's notice. This traces back to holism. When one component of a project goes wrong, the rest suffer as a consequence. Just because you, as a C-suite executive, account for a singular salaried position, doesn't mean the behavior of other workers does not impact you. Everyone needs to perform their best for your business to be a success.

POSITIVE TOLERANCE, NOT TOXIC ENABLEMENT

Nowadays, when people think of building cultures around positivity, it is unfortunately common for their minds to fast-track to "toxic positivity." That is, embracing positive mindsets to the point of neglecting obvious faults in a system or community. While it is pleasant to be showered with compliments even when you step outside in a pair of sweatpants and an old, wrinkled shirt, it obviously doesn't translate to a realistic perception of the wider world will receive you. Take art critiques, for example, many creatives feel shy towards sharing their pieces with others, fearing that they'll be judged harshly or completely shamed. A close friend may not want to give you the frankest criticism, thinking that it'll hurt your feelings, but what will help you improve faster? Shielding yourself from the truth, or facing the reality of what you need to improve on to reach your goals faster?

C-suite executives are the ultimate judges in determining what a company's culture must look like. You tell HR who needs disciplining for infringing on company's policies, set the standards that shape the company's culture. As someone responsible for the success of many other people, it is only responsible that you show little to no tolerance for the disruption of the brand's core values. This does not just extend to glaring infractions, like committing crimes on company property or blatantly breaching company policy. This involves emphasizing company culture in the way you reward and instruct employees. Keeping negative influences on your roster, particularly higher-ups who represent the polar opposite of company values, spells disaster for your company culture. Think of it like how children's behaviour is molded by their guardians because they look to them to learn how to become self-sufficient members of society. If you introduce a new hire in their formative months to short-cutting supervisors who slide them secrets on how to bypass company standards, you'll produce a crop of workers who don't even grasp how to do their job in the "normal" way. Unlike the employees who preceded them, they will only have been exposed to working with the "frugal" mindset, which translates to producing the bare minimum output with the least effort. You don't want to have workers who thrive on "passing grades," especially after spending so long to search for talents that champion the work ethic any company would dream of. You want employees who understand that going above and beyond is what raises your position in the company, and if they hope to see any mobility in relation to their role within the company, they must surpass what is expected of them.

EVERYONE IS A LEADER

Who doesn't love the saying that everyone is in charge of their own destiny? The human mind is imaginative, capable of stretching bounds and reality to craft fantasies worth their own cinematic adaptations (well, some fantasies...most of us would be better off publishing our thoughts in a diary, at best). Dreaming up ambitions is how we motivate yourself to set goal plans, to mold strategies that'll take us to the places we hope to reach in the future.

Yet, many workers feel like unless they hold a managerial position in a company, they aren't fully accountable — not for others, not even themselves. And an employee mustn't be expected to act outside of their job title or compensation, but they mustn't feel inclined to perform as if their contributions only matter if they know someone else is watching. A healthy company thrives on a workforce that is looking to surpass their performance every single day — and unless you decide to compose a company that is almost entirely made up of supervisors, there is no way of managing every single deviation or instance of "slacking off." You must teach your hires to self-manage, that is, be independent.

See how those elementary school learning skills do play an important role in adulthood?

Every capable worker must be a leader. They must be empowered to lead within their span of control. When a manager isn't hovering over their musters, the first instinct mustn't be to slack off and absorb their attention with something other than work; their mindset must be "act like someone is always watching you," except, the goal mustn't be to anticipate material rewards for their behavior. It must be the natural steps to building their reputation in the company, proving themselves as someone who fits into the culture amongst the employees who accomplish their duties without problems.

Of course, your newest hires will need a helping hand to reach this point of self-sufficiency. Companies that have been managing employees for decades can only dream of shaping a workforce that embodies self-sufficient attributes, so you can only imagine the challenges for a new company that has yet to fully form their culture or brand identity. As a C-suite executive, you want to equip your new hires with the tools to perform expertly on their own. Avoid instances where **micromanagement** can creep in — as you may be aware, micromanaging ultimately sabotages the output of employees, rather than increasing it, as is the intention. It is true for both mechanisms and living beings that overwhelming workloads only exhaust the systems that are meant to produce certain results. When someone feels as if they are constantly being spectated for criticisms, they will either have accidents they either wouldn't if they weren't fearful, or neglect to account for mistakes on their own, having become so acclimated to someone else pointing out their faults for them.

A motivated employee is one who believes they are part of something bigger than themselves. Every brand would like to claim they champion a meaningful mission statement, and every prospective hire will claim that your company is the most suited to their altruistic goals — in reality, everyone is looking to derive some advantage out of their professional life, and for employees, it largely boils down to how much satisfaction they derive from their job. Studies have asked employees what they value most about their employment — the money, title, or the job itself. Most answered that they value their job over other factors.

Sounds like an oxymoron when you consider how many cautionary tales exist about averting greed in exchange for happiness. You'd think that a lot of people would cling to superficial measures of success in their professional life, but reality is the opposite. Perhaps this is because prepping yourself for the ideal job requires a discerning mindset: an ability to pursue the right education and experience, to craft the right CV and network with the right people. After surmounting all the steps to get into the dream company, an employee probably won't want to start looking for the next opportunity immediately. Even so-called "job hoppers" seek to get experience out of each role they acquire, which is most feasible when they're working in an environment that supports their personality and ambitions. A capable C-suite executive regularly ensures that the workplace they account for is hospitable; it fulfills employees' needs and does not advertise promises it cannot fulfill.

If you're having trouble finding the right balance between meeting employees' needs and averting total chaos by promising a bunch of benefits that will drive your profits into the ground, put yourself in the perspective of a new hire. Obviously, if someone has unlimited selection of everything and everything they could ask for, their demands will be pretty high, but the average worker doesn't burst into a company accepting the skies and moon to fall into their grasp. Most are just appreciative to be a part of a community that values their input, that has a clear line of communication that makes them feel as if every contribution is valued. If you were to start working at your company today, and even with the "littlest" of responsibilities could feel like you play an important role in a big project, then you've fulfilled your goal. If not, keep chafing the structure to see what can be done to build a better company culture.

There is an optimal formula to analyse the employee retention statistics of a company. Divide the number of employees who have left in each period by the number that still remain, then multiply it by 100. The lower the resulting number, the healthier the company is. If you have a turnover rate that is in the high 90s, for example, not only must you be running some sort of fast-food business to be staying afloat, but you must seriously look at what impersonal values your company embodies to lose employees at such a startling rate.

People like to commit to companies that make them feel like they're being loyal to a cause, that they're not filling their time with something ultimately inconsequential and unnecessary. The stronger your brand and mission statement is, the better it will permeate your workforce to influence a culture of productivity and high achievement.

$$\textit{Employee Retention Rate} =$$

$$\left(\frac{\textit{Number of employees remaining} - \textit{The Number Lost}}{\textit{Number of employees at the Beginning}}\right) \times 100$$

Final Takeaways

Running a company is no easy task. You must optimize so many factors just to sustain the results you're currently seeing; implement new strategies to see upticks in success. Luckily for those who aren't so motivated to give themselves extra work, you can easily trim down the number of problems in your company by optimizing your workforce. This comes from communicating clear expectations with HR, establishing a strong outlook on what an ideal employee must look like, and how your workforce must operate in a standard period. As it turns out, the ultimate predictor of success is holding a clear vision and understanding how to communicate it with others who'll help you achieve your goals. There is no grand conspiracy, no complex, hidden secrets — if it doesn't make practical sense, you'll lose dollars!

Managing Employee Performance

So, you think that you've found your ideal employee roster and are ready to clock out. HR has gotten the credentials reviewed, everyone seems eager to rep your company's mission, and nothing lies ahead but sunshine and rainbows.

In a wishful, alternate reality.

Sadly, we are not in Willy Wonka's Chocolate Factory, or some whimsical, rosy picture of what efficient companies look like. Even once you've found the best-presenting candidates to take the job, your job isn't done, far from it. People slack off. People misrepresent their true qualities.

Your job as a C-suite executive is to minimize the impact of those "defects." To put this into perspective, think of your position like overseeing rail operations. In a world where rail operations are green-lighted to cross tracks that present a million forking pathways. Sounds like a regulatory nightmare, I know, but that is what business can look like from the lens of those in charge. You don't know when the train is about to derail on the dead-end, chipped track. You don't know when you'll have to thrust the engine forward to catch the right track before the barricade goes down, or, on the flip side, when you'll have to slow down your speed to not miss the correct route.

As a C-suite professional, the job never ends. Not when you're doing it right — which, when you're the worker who holds the most power in the company, don't be too surprised that expectations are set a little higher with you. It helps to consider that you can get some pretty nice compensation when you succeed for this reason, too, and maintaining discernment is a sure way to clutch that.

Challenges

You take a glimpse at your quarterly performance metrics and train your other eye on the employee register. It appears that there must be a direct correlation between employee productivity and company successes, but is that the case?

Employee performance is a lot more complex than cursory assessments would let you believe. Obviously, a sharp dip in profits must be a cause for concern, especially if you're seeing suspicious disparities between that and the revenue, perhaps you'll need to have a talk with whoever is managing the books; but internal laundering conspiracies aside, there is a lot you can't determine by analysing employees this way.

For starters, performance management is done to grade ones' statistical metrics, not their growth and development. Let's say that "x" employee started off at an industry high, with project turnarounds that blew the shoes off the senior members at the company, only to, as time passed, taper off in output.

If you were to take a quick glance, that "slip" in performance would still be considered hovering on the better end of internal business metrics. But when you put it against the context in which it hails from, that employee has had an undeniable regression. And that is an undesirable outcome in business, compared to employees who do improve. You don't catch the full impact of "phoned in" work until it reaches its peak: a complete neglect of responsibilities unless it is suspected to bear some consequence on one's job security. An employee who knows that they can elude the eye of HR hawks won't care if they're slacking on aspects of the job, so long as they avoid repercussions.

Meanwhile, an employee who starts off on a shaky foot, yet makes slow strides up to competency, will be identified as a deadweight. Not for the fact that they don't put in effort, but the company will be immediately investing in a professional who doesn't meet the standards for the job. The business world is volatile. We have established that at multiple points in this book, and you're not going to make it far if you're excusing the weaknesses of your team. It's tough to strike a balance between holding employees accountable and measuring expectations for the sake of allowing improvement. If you consider employees as mini-investments, then it is sensible that you'd hold out for one that provides exponential results over time, versus one that declines.

But, for you to even deliberate who's a slump and who shows the promise of a bump, we must define what metrics are used to grade employees.

Key Performance Indicators, shortened as "KPIs," are the standard for which we assess the output of employees. If we look at the quality of restaurants through the grades they are assigned by cuisine experts, we gauge that those grades reflect service, products, and environment.

But the metrics tend to be a lot more narrowed for employees. Just pause for a moment and ask yourself this: how often do you see a supervisor call in an entire department to single out an individual employee? Perhaps, if we're designating employee of the month, because who wouldn't be motivated to model their work output after someone who is reaping recognition (especially if the rewards are more substantial than a ribbon stapled to the suit lapel — we're eying first dibs to the coffee machine).

We don't see managers publicly call out employees who cause turbulence within the work environment. And thank the skies for that, as individual observations may not align with objectivity. If a leader is playing favorites, their gripe with an employee could be because of biases rather than truth.

But there are cases where you enter a workplace where a specific person, if not *specific group* of people's, behavior negatively affects morale.

The *modus operandi* for professionals to manage these rifts is to treat them like loose seams in expensive jeans: nip them quietly, then move on with habit. You're not going to yank at the thread and risk ruining the precious fabric, but you don't want the thread to fling about and tug on more seams, either. It's an issue that must be nipped at the bud, but when you're in public and need to do about your obligations — whatever they may be — are you really going to search for a refined pair of scissors, position yourself in front of a mirror, and carry out the job?

This analogy might sound a bit puzzling, but it reveals a lot about "correctional" methods in workplaces. Leaders in these environments don't want to stir unrest by addressing toxic figures publicly, but they don't want to have anyone dampening their own or others' productivity, either. So, they "quietly" go about handling the situation, and while subtle tugs to the side can help *approach* a problem, it isn't exactly the most assertive method of emphasizing what is and isn't a part of the workplace culture. If you want to highlight role model employees, you put them on display in front of countless others. But what about troublemaker employees? The "independent" players who play for the "me" team, who slide unnecessary jibes at others and plant drama?

Their colleagues may never see them face tangible consequences for their actions. And while that may seem better for the "togetherness" of the workplace, to work through problems without "causing a big ruckus," we set examples through how we hold people accountable for both upstanding and degrading behaviour. Opportunists can identify laxness in a company's discipline as a free pass to bend the rules as much as they want, knowing that they won't face backlash so long as it flies under the "unforgivable" radar.

And no company wants to deal with a culture that radiates "act like someone is never watching" energy. The whole purpose of being a C-suite executive is to mold an environment that propels professionals to be the best professionals they can be!

If only goals were grasped with as much ease as they're drawn. No one aspires for a disordered company, assuming they aren't a double agent planted to drive the operations into ruin, but I'll go ahead and suppose anyone reading this *cares* about the longevity of their business. You want to see productivity reports that show positive outcomes, not people slacking around by the water cooler.

Which begs the question: if so, many companies desire this singular goal, why do so many fall short in producing optimal results?

It'd appear that the person who calls the shots regulates the quality. When you call for professionals that meet a certain standard, the talent market must naturally shape themselves to meet — if not exceed — your expectations. Every company has its own unique mission that'd tweak its responsibilities for employees, but the core values that any strong employee must embody are universal: tenacity, timeliness, and teamwork.

What staggers a lot of companies, particularly the people who oversee the broadest operations within them, from yielding the teams they want, is the metrics they use. Ironically enough, the precise metrics they impose on employees to extract perfection may end up being the decisive blow that stifles it.

Most companies have no process in place to track performance. As is pointed out in multiple other sections of the book, a lot of C-suite executives fail to form leadership that acts on a "proactive" stance rather than a "reactive" one. That is, taking the initiative to avert issues before they fester into major handicaps.

A proactive C-suite executive would institute measures that track employee performance, rather than grade it at a specific period. When you observe a process over an extended period, you generate data that could otherwise be tampered with if extracted from a single point.

If you're not a fan of statistics, don't worry. This isn't a matter of PhD-tier data sets and learning the abstract tool that is the graphing calculator (we're still grasping what the "log" button on standard calculators does). You simply need to practice creating observations that consider an entire portrait — not just the backdrop, or the compelling foreground objects. *The Scream* isn't just a gorgeous work of art because of its glistening moon, but the stars (no surprise!) and thick, dark strokes that creep up the canvas. There is so much more to anything, really, than just the thing itself — we're not isolated from our surrounding environments, and when we study ourselves as products of the culture we're surrounded by, and our continuous habit, we can form a better picture of who we are.

Did we get a little too philosophical there? To simplify this into more relevant terms, an employee's performance must be studied based on how they integrate into their team. How is their performance improving as they spend more time with their colleagues, and do they show weaknesses or improvements when they're thrust into more collaborative projects?

It's important that we judge employees in the context of their teams, because it is often that someone chummies up to interviewers with an amazing story and credentials — then they land the job, squeeze right into the cushy office chair they were looking for, and...fail to stand out at all.

Everyone presents themselves as the best asset a company has ever seen when they're at the recruiting stage. But somehow, when the salary and benefits are in clutch, the talk doesn't seem to match the talent. Why? Are we all pathological liars who'd say anything to climb the trying corporate rungs, or is there perhaps a deeper truth we're neglecting, one flaw that is sabotaging HR professionals worldwide?

If we're to believe that businesses aren't purposefully plundering millions of dollars on failed onboarding processes yearly, then we must consider that a lot of companies follow the wrong template. And that template is evaluating employees from a vantage that is too late and largely too simplistic.

Holism is Proactivity

If you've been paying a good deal of attention throughout this book (which you must — absorbing this information will not only save dollars but make more of them!), you'll realize a common theme is *holism*. That is, analysing a concept as a sum of its parts, rather than separate factors that individually make up a whole.

When a concert is put together, the performance doesn't succeed just because the headliner shows up on stage and does their set. There is so much preparation leading up to the main event, from the dance practices (if we're getting something big budget, we all love our stripped-down acoustic tours as well!) to the stage design to even the lighting practice. So many workers engage in ensuring that the aesthetics line up correctly when they're displayed before the audience — which is why the people in charge do not allow for glaring mistakes up to the deadline. If the engineers responsible for sound, for example, mess up the audio on multiple occasions before the event, who is to say that there won't be a catastrophic error on the big night? That'll lose countless dollars, leaving the compensating parties in a position to lose profits.

Businesses don't have explicit "stage nights," apart from product launches, that'll produce immediate feedback in the marketplace. While this may seem like a relief compared to entertainers whose work all adds up to a single event, businesses can be put in a deceiving comfort because of their lack of focus on continuous evaluations. The reality is that in the competitive world of entrepreneurship, brands are on the clock 24/7 to remain on top. That's why multibillion-dollar brands, with logos that can be recognized by even the most remote of tribes, pay so much in marketing and sponsorships to keep their products talked about. There is no "big day" that you coach your teams to work up to when you're propelling campaigns throughout the year, but there are running assessments by the public that are made or broken by your efforts. When companies fail to address internal issues until they observe a noticeable shift in performance, they don't account for the dynamic nature of public perception.

The grand solution to this? View employee performance as a timeline — not an isolated data point. Employees' growth and regression must be tracked to provide feedback that is tailored to their needs. If someone enters the job with a strong skill set but fails to blend with the environment in their work style, it is important to catch that early on so that they don't end up a deadweight, much worse an extra percentage to your turnover statistics.

Not every employee is going to join your team with the intention of representing the eager attitude they displayed at interviews — but you can assure that they graze that standard by implementing procedures that vet for quality. The reviews mustn't stop at the recruitment stage. The reviews mustn't be diminished to a quarterly annoyance, where workers are ushered into stuffy meeting rooms, lectured by suited figures they've never seen on graphs that've never been shown to them prior to that date.

To integrate people into a culture, you must soak them in it. And that means shaping an environment where the values permeate every aspect of the workplace: from upper management to boots on the ground. Employees are reactive, so if they determine that self-regulation doesn't matter for most of the time, what reason would they have to keep up their best behavior, seeing that people can reap the same (or greater) salary doing much less?

Tangible Rewards

Look at the career opportunities of any company. As you navigate the web page, you'll be confronted with images of beaming faces and workers seemingly fawning over their jobs like they'd just won the lottery.

Companies make work look like fun. And it's understandable why they would. As C-suite executives, you'd only be interested in leading teams full of motivated professionals, people who bring their 110% to the job no matter the conditions. But you tempt the talent market with the best of conditions because you're only interested in serenading the cream of the crop.

Just take a glimpse at Silicon Valley companies, for example. Even the startups will advertise benefits such as day-long snack buffets, on-site gyms, and industry-competitive breaks. Stepping into some of these offices, you'd question if you were stumbling across a luxury spa nestled between the floors or a building meant for work. But the people in charge obviously aren't paying employees to just loll around. For the benefits they provide, they expect to reap returns that are much larger, particularly in productivity and profit.

Many companies struggle to strike the balance between incentivizing employees and lavishing unnecessarily. Remember, business is, in the end, a race to extract the most profit. While every company would love to slap a bunch of grins on their image and project the most wholesomeness, the best way to gratify employees is to provide them secure and rewarding employment. But how can you achieve that when you're not getting the most out of their output?

C-suite executives must be savvy when they're assessing the value of their teams. When employees deliver on what is expected, is there a return on the investment? If you hire a graphic design team to aid the output of your marketing department, yet the performance of the campaign on socials hardly lifts sales, you must validate whether that engagement outweighs the costs. Assuming there was a clear strategy ahead of time, you must've prepared numbers for future dates that would align with the work tied to those hires — if those numbers are missed, then you must reevaluate whether you made the right choice inviting that influx of salaries.

It's like practicing for a competition; prior to the ultimate performance, you're going to need to reach statistics to ensure that you're capable of producing the desired outcome. The best competitors don't grow attached to any strategy, realizing that if they commit to a method that doesn't put them on track of the results, they need to produce by a set date. They will ultimately fall short of victory.

Managing employee performance is a similar concept. As you oversee the revolving door of professionals within your company, you must be mindful of how your employees contribute to producing desirable results. The harsh reality is that a lot of companies tend to over project their value in the marketplace; they see a boom in market interest and assume that the demand justifies gargantuan salary increases that are unsustainable. A business that hires more workers in alignment with market demand must not see strains on their budget, but a leader who doesn't act upon long-term trends, but rather shortsighted observations, will anticipate too much out of a team that can only produce so little.

C-suite executives must prime employees to provide what they were hired for. Nothing more, nothing less. Unrealistic expectations are the foundation of toxic workplaces, and a negative company culture is not conducive to positive outcomes. In fact, for all the labor pressure it exerts, it tends to yield the opposite effect. A C-suite executive that wants to lead a team that is geared for success must know precisely what they're looking for. We've emphasized the point that people with great power hold great responsibility. That ties to how people who make impactful decisions must be aware of what they're demanding.

Imagine if a captain told their crew to go on a voyage with insufficient equipment and supplies. Their crew, understandably, would grow wearied and underperform for the fact they aren't nourished and can't think as well as they would under good oversight. But it's not as if the captain would order that the ship turns around once they're in the middle of the sea and have a mission to accomplish. The workload would continue to strain the crew, lessening their capability to perform standard tasks let alone brace for any setbacks that may arise later.

Businesses face their unexpected setbacks, and they also face their budget constraints that can squeeze a lot of an already overloaded team. As the professionals with the most oversight in the company, it's essential the C-suite executives show awareness and aptitude; they must know when they're asking more of employees than they were responsible for on the job, to determine if workers are falling short on their responsibilities, or in actuality, underperforming due to imbalanced expectations.

More than that, C-suite executives must have a clear plan from the get-go that considers the capabilities of their team, and what their production can afford in terms of extra help and the brand's expansion. There is no harm in ambition; that is the root of impactful businesses, and an unimaginative C-suite executive will never take their team far. In fact, the most diligent professionals would like to affiliate themselves with a company that strives for constant growth. That is why brands like Apple and Google are the most sought out amongst young tech graduates, and why companies that stagnate in their image and catalogue tend to taper off in not only public perception, but also talent interest, regardless of the quality of their offerings.

What does hurt companies is a lack of awareness. And if you're setting yourself up for goals that are beyond the average reach of competitors, you must account for the level of preparation it'll take to fulfill that ambition. That'll track employees on a road for success that is accurate and realistic.

Plan the Necessary Resources

Drawing back on our earlier analogy about planning for voyages, business leaders must be intentional about how they supply their workers for success.

Employees, financially, aren't just immediate profit gains. They need infusions of resources to grow and thrive. Think of the costs to train a single employee. No matter how qualified an individual is, whether they've interned for a sister company before they landed a job or did the switch from a completely unrelated industry, they'll undergo an onboarding process. The time to integrate an employee can range anywhere from a couple of days to several weeks, and while companies will seek professionals who'll learn their expectations faster, no results come instantaneously.

Financially, businesses must be acutely aware of the financial pros and cons of expanding. Employees are an investment, a strategic choice to grow a company, but to see upward strides in the business world, you'll need money.

How many businesses attribute their failures to poor financial decisions? When you look at poor outcomes in the employee productivity sphere, a lot of issues boil down to poor planning. You can court dozens of promising professionals into your company, but if you don't properly outline the financial costs, then at least one department is doomed to disorder (sorry, accounting!).

Similarly, C-suite executives must be prepped to make the best investments for the longevity of their company. That sometimes means bracing for expensive decisions that'll ultimately reap large successes. It's important to emphasize that this does *not* mean plunging headfirst into a massive splurge, because your responsibility to your workers is to ensure their job security, and blowing company resources is a surefire way to risk that.

What C-suite executives must be doing is educating themselves on the resources necessary to mold an effective team. They must be diligently partnering with HR to make the best hiring — and training — processes happen. If the current onboarding process isn't yielding desirable results, it's high time that you pull the brakes and consider whether your methods are outdated. Some traditions must be phased out, and what works for a mid-sized company won't mesh with a large one.

It's evident that a lot of diligent management boils down to awareness and collaboration — the C-suite can be an alienating position, isolating professionals in that role from the needs of the rest of a company. As rewarding as it can be to lead a company, C-suite executives mustn't be deceived by the lavishes and privileges — you'll need to, using your own initiative, take a step down at times to see the inner workings of other departments. It's through these observations that you'll embody a leadership that represents the needs of the people you lead. Communication is an asset to extracting the best performance out of HR, and as a (positive!) consequence, the workers they let on.

The key to optimizing your role as a C-suite executive is to keep one principle in mind: tie people to dollars, and dollars to the boots on the ground. If financing a certain management choice doesn't make sense, it must be abandoned. Overseeing employees requires a mindset that prioritizes taking the most financially savvy decisions possible. That goes from hiring talents with reasonable rates to integrating them in the company culture with a seamlessness that respects resources and expectations.

Internal Discord Seeps into the End Product

Anyone who says they're eager to sign up for a toxic work environment is a liar. Or they're willing to overlook a certain number of negatives if it'll pay off in the long run — but what everyone learns from enduring poor management is that no amount of money can make a badly run workplace sustainable.

Conflicts are part and parcel of the workplace. As much as we emphasize bringing professionalism to professional environments, the reality is that when you put a bunch of people together, you're bound to draw out the worst and best elements of their personality. Add stress, and the scale tips more towards the negative.

Pressure is natural in a space that places high expectations upon people. Training for a competition, athletes don't imagine that they'll be slurping milkshakes while they laze out on the couch until the deadline, but they can't fully brace for the strain of their practices, either. Pushing yourself to become a more "evolved" individual is hard, and workplaces demand of workers to seek growth every single day. That brews feelings of envy, possessiveness, and sometimes, bold hatred.

You don't walk into a retail store expecting the employees to hug or put on a family show. Ideally, personalities within a team must be in sync with each other, but what the customer cares most about is being provided a pleasant experience, and that's why employers coach their workers to give off welcoming qualities. As much as interviewers vet for collaborative qualities; however, anyone can vouch for the disparity in collaboration between different work environments. Some workplaces have a handle on shoving drama down before it rushes to the forefront of the business. Some neglect these issues until they trickle all the way down to the boots on the ground, and that's when it slips to customers.

In many industries, boots on the ground are, to some degree, the unsaid spokespersons for their employers. When a retail customer steps into a store, their experience with the workers will impact their image of the brand. If they witness disorganization in either the store setup or ease of service, they won't be motivated to patronize the brand again. With dozens of brands cropping up each day, who's going to wait for an established entity to pick up their act when they could seek competency elsewhere? First impressions are everything, and as much as we can mourn people's unwillingness to explore beyond surface-level representation, you can't scrutinize people you're asking for money.

This doesn't just apply to in-store experiences. The boots on the ground for a manufacturing company can make or break the reputation. In this year alone, there have been numerous recalls in the food industry. A cold brew company has faced a major contamination at their factories, halting production and inevitably fracturing their partnerships with major contractors.

Are contamination incidents the result of workers gossiping too much at the assembly lines? Not necessarily, but when you have a hazardous incident that stems from improper hygiene practices, that reflects a lack of care amongst workers. Workers must be informed to wipe equipment so that it doesn't pick up particles from other substances. Cross contamination is a result of negligence, which is the mark of a workplace caught in discord.

As you can predict, the major incidents that arise from negligence cost companies a lot of dollars. Just put yourself in the shoes of the contractors that were affected by the manufacturing issues. Not only do they have to public to amend with for their stained reputation, but they also can't rely on a contract that has proven to not meet standards that were outlined in the clauses. The manufacturing company would lose their dependency in the industry, toppling down the rungs so that competitors who avoid these missteps take their place. It's the reality of the business that one accident can fester to a widespread disaster; when you ask of a bunch of people to patronize your services, you can't be surprised when a bunch of eyes are privy to every mistake you make.

All of this is to highlight that employees don't write the company values or plan the branding like upper management might do. Regardless, they have a strong impact on how those strategies land with the public. When employees aren't vetted to align with brand values, they will tarnish the company's reception amongst the public. How much this will negatively impact the company's reputation depends on their existing influence and the severity of the consequences. Since small rifts can sum up to huge disasters, you can't necessarily predict the gravity of an issue based on whether employees are engaging "petty workplace conflicts" or serious crimes or taking place under your supervision.

No matter the degree to which internal company conflicts have escalated, C-suite executives must encourage procedures that quash them before they fester. They say it takes only a small while before a negative behavior grows into a habit, and it's harder to train people to embody upstanding behaviour than it is to allow them to slump into human instincts. We're naturally defensive, prone to assumption and rebellion. But in a professional environment, there's no place for primitive tendencies. Only professionalism must be accepted.

Dismissing Bad Players

Every industry has its issues with calling out internal problems. It's natural to communities in general to form "defenses" around those who must be shunned for their toxic behavior, rather than embraced for the other positive qualities they're deemed to bring.

The entertainment industry is perhaps the most prominent, if not glaring, example of this. The surge of the #MeToo movement cast a light on the ugly side of Hollywood, wherein multiple men avoided accountability for the fact that they held powerful relationships with others that shielded them. This ironclad protection interfered with justice for serious crimes and contributed to work environments that compromised the safety of vulnerable individuals.

Watching the scandal unfold, it may seem ridiculous to an outsider that such a powerful industry, let alone one that exists in the graces of public perception, would let so many malicious personalities fly under the radar. Wouldn't billion-dollar studios want to avert lawsuits by cutting off these people as soon as they caught wind of reports? Wouldn't they diligently vet for predators so that they wouldn't risk the wellbeing of their invested talents?

You'd think that disciplinary practices would be seriously upheld in the richest of companies, because they have so much on the line in the event of a failure. But when we turn the lens on multiple other businesses, we see that the act of vetting a workplace's internal culture is much rarer than it must be.

A lot of leaders in these environments ignore toxic workers because they produce unit. They move sales, bring in a lot of dollars or patrons. When you look at an industry like Hollywood, almost all the "excused" predators had strong connections or successful film records. It's an unfortunate trend for companies to turn a blind eye on workers that make up for poor personality traits in productivity, neglecting the performance of others and being forced to silence themselves as a result. In a business, the boots on the ground collectively hold a lot of power, but as individual workers, they are powerless against the whims of upper management. Thus, they risk being exposed to abusive behavior that exploits how little power they hold in the business structure.

Hollywood is one of many industries that have managed to get away with allowing toxicity under the table: signing deals with shady actors and silencing vulnerable groups who come forward with stories. But if there is one silver lining to the #MeToo movement — a glimmer of hope, as well as an important lesson for business leaders — it is that no business, no matter how powerful it may be, is invulnerable to the consequences of negligent employee management. When you breed a toxic workplace culture, you're not only exposing powerless employees to the poison, you're slowly dosing your business, until the problem boils over and reaches the eyes of the public. At that point, you can't contain the controversy. Just look at the catastrophe that has arisen from toxic food production business where employees aren't given breaks to use the washroom or rest. These poor practices result in hygienic and quality issues that affect the end product that is displayed on shelves to the public. And when people see themselves being victimized by your business's negligent practices, it is no longer just a "small downside" for employees to digest and overlook. It is a widespread controversy that can tarnish your brand irreversibly.

Obviously, it must go without saying that abusive behaviour like harassment must be corrected regardless of its potential to alight the flames of public criticism. Businesses have a moral responsibility to their employees, and this keeps with meeting the expectations you draw out to talents when you hire them — no worker must put up with burdens that they didn't sign up for.

The glum reality, however, is that a lot of businesses do think in a profit-first mentality; that's how these enabling cultures arise, and why we must ground the importance of snuffing out toxicity when it's reported. Too many C-suite executives, and members of upper management in general tend to overlook the flaws of "favorites" who garner powerful connections within the company. Either these protected individuals produce a significant number of units for the company, or they've somehow slid into the favor of powerful individuals. We've spoken on the failings of nepotism, of considering employees for traits outside of what they tangibly contribute to the job due to irrelevant biases. Vetting toxicity in the workplace is tantamount to ending unproductive practices. If you want to raise a field of competent workers, then you must place them under leadership that cares for their growth. A beautiful flower won't blossom under dim conditions, but place the seedling in the right environment, and it'll sprout just as intended.

Money Isn't Everything

This header might come as a surprise given the lessons that have been championed throughout the book You want to be a financially savvy leader in the C-suite, but at the same time, you mustn't prioritize profits. What? That sounds like a contradiction in and of itself, but what if I told you, it's conducive to supporting a sustainable business?

Consider this scenario: you've decided to review your employees, and have HR look at the workers who've provided the lowest output in the last quarter. Their assessment returns a list of a dozen workers, and all of them hired at different times, but share one common characteristic. They aren't meeting the level of productivity that you'd like.

You could just go ahead and fire the underperforming employees. At the end of the day, you've placed a bar, and these people have yet to grasp, let alone raise their heads above it. If they're falling short of their peers, they must be filed as deadweight and let go.

Or must they?

As we've learned throughout this section, tracking employment performance is a long process, one that accounts for multiple, broad factors. You need to analyse their contributions in many regards, and that includes the way they approach work. If you're a C-suite executive overseeing workers, your job is a team endeavor, meaning their qualities stretch beyond what they're individually capable of. How they impact the performance of others can tell a lot about their level of output.

To expand on this, let's return to the consequences of toxic work environments. Poorly managed stores in retail are known to have high rates of turnover, and supervisors aren't looking to bleed talent that they've invested resources into training. A huge wound in these workplaces' success is the fact that they don't cultivate employees that are motivated for the job. If someone enters an environment where they're pressured to generate results at a high capacity yet are surrounded by factors that only hinder their labor, they aren't just going to be tugged away from the standard — they'll be pulled to a bar far below their capabilities.

Workers must be independent thinkers. A good employee is one that knows to take initiative even when they're not guaranteed to take recognition; this is a basic value we've been taught since elementary school: do what is asked even when no one is looking. But humans are not robots, which means that we can't produce perfect results like we're chained to an algorithm. Whether we'd like to be or not, we're influenced by our environment, and the harsher you allow your workplace conditions to be, the more inevitable it is there will be mishaps and disastrous errors.

If you've started to notice this bears similarities to the former section, you're indeed correct — assessing a workplace's toxicity must be considered when evaluating an underperforming employee. It's easy to write someone off as a bad investment and look to greener pastures, but when training costs grow and retention rates descend through the floor, you'll wish you paused and recalibrated your management practices.

Look for warning signs before it is too late. Sometimes, the employee is to blame, as not everyone will be a correct fit for your company's culture, even if the future looked promising in the interview stage. Other times, you may be missing flaws in your internal structure that drive productivity down. An employee that is eager to learn and collaborate must never be falling short of standards.

Feedback Must Be like a 24/7 Walk-in Clinic

Career coaches are gaining popularity with young professionals. The industry might seem frivolous at first glance, because who needs to pay another individual to tell them how to approach their job, especially when they aren't privy to the ins-and-outs of their workplace?

To this, I advise you to dive deeper, because when you study the market, it's evident that these contractors fill a gaping demand.

To define this phenomenon through a real-world connection, look at the surge in millennials taking their doctor checkups seriously. A lot of adults have historically neglected the importance of monitoring their health not just as mandated in childhood — but rigorously as a part of their daily regimen. Of course, no one is expected to strut into the doctor's office every weekend like it's a spare room in their home, but as people learn the dramatic consequences of silent illnesses, they've become vigilant about routine checkups to ensure they catch conditions before they become difficult to treat.

Employee management is a lot like being vigilant about your health. You can pass on the regular doctor's appointment because you don't have enough time or would simply rather send your focus to other endeavors; but by doing so, you risk letting problems grow that'd escape the naked eye.

To go even further than that, there are a lot of subtle signs of internal problems that people neglect not because they don't notice them, because they wager the nuisance of addressing them outweighs the possibility it'll "go away on its own."

Sometimes, problems do just disappear with time. Adults in a company, for example, must be capable of resolution without authority involvement.

Yet, matters don't often feather away so simply. And that's why we've observed the rise of career coaches; young professionals are seeing that they could reap greater prospects in the job market with the counsel of a second voice but fail to find that guidance in the workplace. How many companies will rigorously coach you to improve once you're hired? Generally, the expectation is that you pass through three stages: first, the interview, to identify how much support you'll need to assimilate into the culture, and afterwards, the onboarding process that is often shaped impersonally and to target as much workers as possible. You may get a couple of tips from your supervisors afterwards if it's requested, but otherwise, you're expected to independently figure out your own weaknesses and strengths.

Until your weaknesses prove too burdensome for business.

Managers' tendency to retroactively pass judgement onto employees — that is, informing them of faulty methods only after it causes troubles for the business — prevents workers from correcting their behaviour before it costs them severely. A lot of managers don't care to write off new hires as a loss and churn them out until they find new recruits that satisfy standards just well enough.

If you're in a fast-paced market that constantly has new trends moving in, like retail, the costs of rotating hires might not be as high as a startup business. This mentality wouldn't hold up in an industry like tech, where the learning gap to learn companies' preferred coding styles and such demands extensive labor.

$$Cost\ Per\ Hire = \frac{Total\ Recruiting\ Costs}{Number\ of\ Hires}$$

Generally, it is preferable that an employer grows employees than fetching a bunch of burgeoning talents. You invite skilled people to use your resources in exchange for them multiplying the assets you have at your disposal. When a business attracts a high turnover rate, they're burning more than they could with a sustainable team.

C-suite executives must be encouraging managers at all levels to assign feedback regularly. Don't call employees for the odd meeting, when they'll be accustomed to drifting through work without regard for quality or growth. Remind them that feedback is a standard — not a rarity — and if they want to integrate into the culture, they must adopt growth-aligned practices.

Once you standardize feedback, you'll notice that the workers that want to "go through the motions" get swiftly weeded out. Slackers won't desire an environment where they're constantly watched for change, especially if they are overwhelmed with attitudes that embody this trait. Talents who actually want to hone their skills as professionals will appreciate a workplace that presents constant opportunities for improvement. Even if a professional isn't seeking long-term employment, they can predict they'll be leaving the environment as a more capable individual than they were when they arrived. That is an extra benefit you're providing to them free of charge — and the cherry on the cake is that you'll be able to profit off it as well!

Opportunities

We've gotten a glimpse of the setbacks that can affect effective employee management. As is true with all problems in the business world, there are solutions that can prevent failures; but, to produce successes, you must create a model that primes your management proactively.

Evaluating the Performance Management Program

Do you have an ongoing program where you are receiving regular feedback and coaching? A telltale sign of a fragmented company is poor communication between the farthest levels. The outcomes of the boots on the ground must be not just made aware to C-suite but considered and met with feedback.

No, it mustn't be expected that C-suite executives draft detailed blueprints for each one of their workers. The purpose of having different levels of management is to delegate leadership to a broader group, and ideally, the supervisors you have on the ground will be supplying them with that feedback. But for them to do so successfully, you must have a process in place to account for growth.

What does the review process look like in your company? Is it a seasonal practice, tailored to isolated discussions or voiced in sizable meetings? How are roundtable discussions at the highest levels reflected in changes on the floor?

Although C-suite executives are ultimately responsible for the success of a company, a company is beholden to more than its direct leaders — stakeholders, too, have a right to input in a business's direction. Are their concerns shifting the trajectory of the business?

Stakeholders, like managers, are not a monolith. They may present different beliefs that stem from their differing reasons to invest in a cause. Some are driven to support a business because they are in alignment with their mission. In that case, you'd expect that they seek strategies that reflect the principles they got on board for. Others will join in on the journey because they predict massive potential for growth. These stakeholders will want to see ambitious plans, a hunger for change and expansion.

You can very well have conflicting views on what your business must do to propel itself to a higher level. And while it's great to bask in the mantra of following your heart and despite the opinions of others, business isn't a happy-go-lucky piece of media — powerful entities' interests are on the line, and when you have other's finances at stake, the consequences for taking a faulty decision are far-reaching.

To consolidate all these points, ensure that you facilitate a feedback process that considers all the influences that must impact employee performance. Reception amongst the public, synergizing with colleagues, individual productivity, and adhering to company standards are the main qualities that would be assessed in a worker. If someone falls short in any one of these categories, you may extract observations that not only put them on track to modelling better behavior but can help others who are struggling to meet company expectations. This continuous feedback "catches" those who fall behind while motivating those at the front of the pack to keep striding up to new heights.

Acknowledge Criticisms in a Timely Manner

Smaller companies tend to struggle less with the employee-to-management feedback process. Because the teams are tight, the complaints of a boot on the ground have a greater chance of reaching those at the top of the chain compared to a large company. You don't imagine that the CEO of Disney will hear that you're disgruntled by a coworker in the animation department, even if that coworker is showing extremely toxic behavior. The CEO simply has too many responsibilities to account for to deliberate HR complaints. That's why they assign professionals to handle conflicts before they leak into catastrophes that will reach their level either through public criticism or massive internal backlash.

In some ways, having employees as resources to support other employees can be an advantage. A C-suite won't be equipped to deal with the breadth of issues you'd encounter in a large business, although they'd have better prospects for approaching this at a smaller scale. In small businesses, the teams are so small that you can have a tight control over maintaining a specific culture.

But even as you grow and delegate responsibilities to more people, you must be mindful of the fact that you are ultimately responsible for more workers' outcomes. The mini leaders you build up must be vigilant about addressing challenges that employees report to them, as that'd be your priority if you were in their position.

Sadly, the imperativeness of this task isn't understood by every authority in business. A lot of supposed leaders take their power as an excuse to slack off, either because they're numb to consequences or haven't been primed to identify them in their formative stages.

As the leader amongst leaders, C-suite executives must breed a culture that encourages early action. When employees report toxicity in the environment, it mustn't be a lengthy process to see changes be made. That is the deadly precursor to disasters where companies enable issues that could've been avoided with greater vigilance. How many times have we witnessed news articles that shine a light on this frustrating scenario? Rich companies with so many resources, so many talented leaders at their disposal, somehow fail to resolve internal issues that you wouldn't expect to see at that level.

Unfortunately, success isn't always a sign of capability. Sometimes businesses grow too big for their skillset, and a magnified light of their inner workings exposes the reality of their operations: dysfunction and disorganization.

You don't want to be the brand that is smeared by avoidable mistakes. You don't want to be the employer that repels talented professionals because your reputation is in the gutters. A good C-suite executive represents a brand that leaves a positive impression on the market; the opposite is achieved when your controversy precedes your offerings (assuming your offerings aren't the cause of controversy itself).

To wrap this into a digestible lesson, don't view feedback as a one-way process — take it as it's received from groups outside of the C-suite. When employees pass on complaints to their managers, there must be immediate steps to address those challenges. Pressures are a natural part of being a part of an environment with high expectations, but when similar criticisms continue to be vocalized, it might be time to change your approach.

Drop the 90-Day Culture

A lot of companies follow a 90-day culture for evaluations. This standardized time frame allows for a breadth of time between assessments, and for both leaders and their workers to know when it is time to see the culmination of their hard work.

While having a set deadline for a process can seem helpful, it can actively encourage performative behavior. Understandably, you can argue that working is a performance in itself. Acting like you are immensely productive until the clock reaches closing time, except you are compensated to orchestrate a level of diligence.

A counterpoint would be that while C-suite executives want employees to present their best image at work, they do desire professionals who have an innate "aptitude" in their skillset. No, you can't vet every single talent that shows up at your door to assure excellence, but you will want to skim the candidates who show an obvious disinterest in fulfilling the job outside of what they'll get backlash for.

Which is where the issue with 90-day evaluations comes from because the window of time is fixed, it doesn't allow for malleability or sincerity. You know when the results will arrive, and that stunts growth when it doesn't adhere to the corporate idea of perfection.

Compare this to food safety assessments. Every restaurant (one type of business!) must undergo inspections carried out by certified inspectors. These inspectors will announce beforehand that they are showing up within a broad window of time, but not only can consumers report concerns at any day of the year, but inspectors can anonymously act upon observations that fall below their guidelines.

This flexible enforcement of feedback holds restaurants to a safe standard. Which is important, because imagine if greedy business owners decided to cut corners when they knew inspectors weren't in their vicinity? The same lax mentality can be bred amongst workers if they don't detect an urgency to improve, which is why you must foster a system that informs workers that performance is continuously being assessed. If a 90-day window is too long for the industry you serve, don't feel compelled to uphold that. Different seasons present different expectations, and so will the mission your company is striving to uphold. There is no one-fits-all standard for the diverse array of businesses our world has to offer.

Always Document Challenges — AND WINS!

We all have areas that we can grow. Our culture has begun to have more conversations about the harm of "toxic positivity," wherein environments become insular bubbles that clashing discourse is snuffed.

No one wants to be trapped in a cycle of sameness. But when you reduce yourself to the temporary comfort of stagnation, due to fear of the temporary pains of improvement, then you'll inadvertently trap yourself in these dishonest echo boxes. This is often the foundation of workplace cultures that reject criticism and cling to destructive behaviors. Ironically, an obsession with pushing self-congratulatory behavior can empower those in charge while brutally taking down those who aren't.

On the other hand, embracing criticism can also fuel its own extremes. We want to acknowledge the places that employees can grow, but what strengths can they play off? A good teacher will communicate with a student through their *lingua franca* — that is, communicating in a way that they can grasp and build on. If you approach someone with a critical attitude, they'll instinctively feel slightly defensive about their capabilities. No competent leader wants to form an environment where their peers feel doubtful of their potential to drive success; when the dialogue leans to pessimistic, it may come across as them being insufficient to producing positive results.

As with every aspect of life, balance is the key to harmony. Mesh your critiques with positive notes that can motivate employees to sustain certain behaviours. Does one employee fall short on productive output, but is noted as a great person to collaborate with? Emphasize how they're a positive influence on their colleagues, but individually must look to others for a model on how to amp up their performance. You'll see that workers team together to bring out the best qualities in themselves, which is far preferable to a hostile environment that's steeped in competition.

Be Invested in the Employees' Success

Employees are some of a company's most valuable assets, but not every C-suite executive understands how to respect this principle.

You can't retain every single employee or turn them into a superstar, but you can maximize unimaginable returns out of a team when you optimize them for success.

Business leaders who have a good understanding of their workers will put them on a trajectory to win. This entails learning their goals and equipping them to achieve them. How strong is communication in your company? Naturally, the number of divisions and numbers in your workforce can complicate the understanding process, but that is no excuse to isolate yourself from taking accountability.

At the end of the day, C-suite executives are responsible for overseeing the success of their business's mission. Employees are a huge part if not integral to making achievements possible. The highest authorities in a company must strive daily to align workers with the recipe for success. Ensure that the general output is meeting a baseline standard, and that over an extended stretch of time, productivity is showing heightened outcomes, rather than signs of regression.

Despite the affiliations of entrepreneurship with independence, overseeing a business is the ultimate test of teamwork. Any leader who thinks that they're "too big" to relate to the struggles and needs of employees will ultimately fail to resonate with their growth, thereby failing to build a roster of talents who out-compete market rivals.

Don't be the business that is out of touch. Attune yourself to the resounding opinion.

Upper Management must Grasp the Impact of their Directions

As much as you'll endeavor to implement decisions that bring positive effects to the boots on the ground, the truth of life is that everything produces positive and negative effects. Especially because a lot of tailoring your standards for success is an experimental, highly individualized process, you can't expect for every plan to land perfectly upon launch.

C-suite executives must look to understand how the standards they introduce bring both positive and unintended shifts to the workplace. If there are consequences to a new change that you suggested, what are they, and is the weight of these consequences excusable? Sometimes, you must weigh the good with the bad, but you can't ignore the dichotomy altogether. By practicing awareness of the impact of your leadership, you'll proactively diminish your contributions to stagnated growth, underperformances and PTO.

Evaluate the Employee with a Whole Mindset

Assess your employees as a sum of all their contributions: what they add to the team, and if relevant, what they take away. Eventually (or at least if you're savvy, you'll aim for this eventuality), your brand's reputation will attract the cream of the crop in terms of talents. But just because a worker is considered generally skilled within the landscape you're competing in, doesn't mean that all the assets they provide are desirable for your purposes.

Take tech startups, for example. A lot of stakeholders have had to pressure C-suite executives to explicitly search for candidates who possess experience outside of the field, due to the personality clashes that tend to come with results-driven professionals.

Someone can be an amazing producer, but not so efficient in the scheme of collaborating with others. As we've mentioned that a business is one big team project, you'll want to deliberate how that worker can enhance their skills in the area that conflict with their colleagues. Neglection to do so is how workplaces turn into toxic environments — you don't want to miss out on nurturing amazing talents because of weaknesses that can be easily averted.

Progressive Discipline

Keep on Top of Observations

Ensure that you document issues in a timely manner, keeping a watch on when they need to be disciplined and corrected.

The process of remodeling employee's behaviors must be rehabilitative — not intended to pass on punishment.

Remember that your workers are assets that you want to encourage to, in the long run, present their best performances for. Actively discouraging them will only diminish loyalty and stifle discussion, which is the opposite of what you want when you're facilitating feedback.

Instituting a clear process for feedback will allow for managers to assess employees with ease, as well as take sincere action outside of the observational stage. The feedback cycle mustn't end with the employee simply being told where they must improve. Are you outlining steps that can be actively followed to produce better results? Are you drawing plans to rehabilitate aspects of the workplace that aren't conducive to productivity?

Take the Journey Step by Step

Success isn't a race; the illusion of winning is. The brands that stay on top are the ones that maintain longevity, and despite the ease with which they may appear to dominate the market, they're led by professionals who've meticulously laid the foundation for long-term prosperity.

If this sounds like the ingredient list for a 12-tier cake, don't worry, we're not speaking of geniuses who have become fluent in the arcane. The key ingredients to longevity are a lot simpler than you'd imagine, but they do require a lot of time to fester.

As a business leader, you must approach the process of raising employee performance as an extensive project. Exercise patience and mindfulness. Teams won't evolve overnight, but with consistent oversight, you can lay the groundwork for a sustainable success story.

KEY TAKEAWAYS

Mastering the art of productivity optimization is hard for any leader, even if they're the highest-ranking member of a business. C-suite executives can feel overwhelmed by the dynamic landscape of employees' performance. Some will take far longer to adopt certain techniques than others, and even if you vet for candidates that embody industrious qualities, there is a lot of learning on the job to occur.

Remember that your workers are an investment, and the more resources you put towards smart coaching, the larger a return you can expect in your business's success.

Results are rarely immediate. If you plan to aggressively scale your business, the process will be taxing, but not fast yielding. That's why multiple companies stagnate at the mid-sized stage, if not completely fail at protecting their position in the market altogether. Half of the challenge is simply operating your business at an extent that maintains relevancy, never mind the strain of striving for greater heights in a notoriously unforgiving industry.

As the most powerful leaders within a business, C-suite executives must be mindful that there are so many factors that go into meeting the standards of optimal performance, and gearing employees to sustain that is an enduring battle. You can't expect to set up the policies and leave workers to overcome their struggles as they arise. There will always be new problems that crop up, and new improvements to suggest as you draft new goals. Keeping a consistent line of communication for feedback will motivate a culture that is grounded in priming workers for long-term success.

Employee Engagement & Morale

In this book, we've dived into the schematics behind optimizing your HR to boost employee productivity. Sounds like a tall order when you're not equipped with the right tools to achieve it. Let's be honest, we've *all* as C-suite executives seen the ups and downs of shaping a business, whether it be through shadowing someone we've taken over, or absorbing the consequences ourselves.

Navigating the world of business isn't easy. I know, I know, we've stressed this point in the book so many times it might as well become a slogan, but if you have any firsthand knowledge of this industry, you'll know there's no immediate path to success. You'll realize that because the path is so tough, and so extensive, that you must perfect your steps along the way to ensure that you don't take a sharp detour. It's bad enough when the ride trudges along at a slower pace than anticipated. It's disastrous when you're thrown off the rails, veering from a one-way trip to Boston to a sudden trip to Appalachia.

When it comes to collaborative processes, acing the goals boils down to honing the team. All the introverted souls will be crushed at this, because how many people strove for a C-suite position thinking that at the top, they'll finally *not* be beholden to anyone else?

Sorry to inform, but the corporate world is one big, gigantic group project. And we all know what group projects were like in school. You could get paired with the slackers, the geniuses, or the procrastinators, but one thing that'd unite any crop of kids on a task was strong leadership. You, as the *head in charge*, the professional everyone responds to, and looks up to must be setting the groundwork for success. It's fun to whip up an ambitious vision in your mind and expect everyone to follow suit from giving off "vibes," but your employees aren't psychics, and people don't normally push themselves for excellence.

...which begs the question. How do you motivate dozens, if not hundreds of people to exert themselves even when you're not hovering over them? We may be in the digital age, but there's no technology that'll allow you to monitor every step of your employee's work performance. Evaluations will largely be collected by your responding managers, and even of that group, who's going to check that *they're* hustling once the clock is running?

We've spoken about fostering an environment where workers feel incentivised to vet one another, and report behaviour that hinders productivity. We've touched on the consequences of narrow-sighted hiring practices, and how fixating on a certain type of candidate can constrain the potential of your workforce.

Let's imagine that you, the reader, have applied the counsel from the prior sections. You're beaming in your office, seeing the glimmers of a new path forged ahead.

Your employees are on track for greatness. HR has started to field in the best crop of applicants, and it's raining money outside.

Okay, the last part is a bit too imaginative. You likely won't start raking in the cash instantly, and that's the satisfying part of the ultimate payoff. By delaying gratification, that is, keeping your head low until a series of actions accumulate in a bigger result, you get to reap the riches of your efforts after a long grind.

It's a common line of advice, and for how often it appears in motivational books, you'd think that every human being would live to that mantra.

But most don't.

Most employees won't.

Before you panic, this isn't to say that the cubicle B must be humoring a food fight when copying when typing up the spreadsheet gets too dull. Employees are obligated to provide an asset while they're being paid; meaning that when a professional is on the clock, you're in your right to expect that they're meeting a minimum standard for their financial compensation.

Most workers aren't showing up at the office to repurpose it as a jungle gym. But naturally, when you commit someone to a repetitive, often tolling task for a number of hours, they're going to get worn out. When people are wearied, their motivation declines.

As the head disciplinarian for productivity, you don't want to see motivation plummet. Because despite how much we like to sermonize about the importance of rigor, giving your 100% even when you're feeling more at a 30% (or lower, if that bed you woke up on was super wonky) — workers are humans, not robots.

At least, not yet. Or I'd predict that not being applicable to your business since you're consulting this book. Human psychology hacks probably aren't of much use to an unemotional machine, but who are we to estimate the bounds of AI (that's way out of our wheelhouse!)?

What we *do* know is that thriving businesses sustain a high level of output. Their internal leadership must be able to hold their employees to an-above-industry average of productivity. When that fails to occur, they'll lose their advantage in the market, and no business manages to capture (let alone maintain) a complete monopoly. There is always a competitor, another brand full of hungry professionals that won't hesitate to swoop in and snatch your crown.

So, how do you prevent the coup and fan the flames of resolve in your workforce?

The answer is summed up in one word — engagement.

What is Engagement?

If you've ever picked up one of those tomes off the library shelves that read like they've crammed in every word in the English Dictionary, you'd know that it's hard to grasp a concept when you don't understand the underlying parts. The cruel authors who brandish tongue-twisters every sentence seem to delight in this, but in this book, we want you to follow along with the lessons we're teaching.

That's why we're presenting you with a simple and concise definition of a word you've probably encountered before, although you might have not in this context.

Employee engagement encompasses the tactics you use to sustain momentum. As a C-suite executive, you must be extremely *tactical*, thinking up and executing strategies at every turn. Engagement is but one space you'll be homing in on.

Potlucks, games, socials — these are all displays of employee engagement. The interrelating thread is that all these activities link workers with the brand's mission. They aren't simply treated like distinct pieces in an overly large jigsaw puzzle; they're connected to a core cause, reinforced through outreach initiatives.

$$\mathit{Employee\ Engagement\ Score} = \left(\frac{\mathit{Number\ of\ Engaged\ Employees}}{\mathit{Total\ Number\ of\ Employees\ Surveyed}}\right) \times 100$$

It's a common truth in life that people feel more attached to a project's success when they're to benefit from it. Say that someone got a job promotion, for example — if they're your colleague, you'll probably congratulate them because you look fondly back on memories of hustling late-night in the cubicles. If they're a friend, you'll be even more attached to their success. This is someone you have a deep relationship with, as their happiness transfers to you.

But what if this promoted individual was a complete stranger? The Joe that passes by you every walk to work on a Monday, who you maybe exchange glances with but never explicitly acknowledge?

Maybe you'll think it's cool to see someone else propel themselves upwards in life. We're not hopelessly enviable creatures, at least not all of us. Though, I don't think it'd be rude to assume that most of us would be entirely indifferent to the news.

Hard work breeds success, and it's impressive to see anyone approach the echelons of human achievement. We've seen the fanfare surrounding big-name brands, athletes, and other sorts of worldly superstars. But outside of these bubbles of starry-eyed craze, there are a lot of people who are either jealous or uncaring of these occurrences. Call it rude, but if someone has no vested interest in another's accomplishment, then is there really a reason for them to indulge it besides a cursory "congratulations?"

At the end of the day, an employee is tied to your business by contract. They don't see the quarterly profits. They don't attend all the shareholder meetings, and they likely don't negotiate much of the contracts you'll be signing.

C-suite executives seek out talents based on the skills they bring towards a specific need. Professionals aren't expected to be all-rounders, friends, or support groups. They're expected to bring a surplus in output, and so long as that dynamic is material, we can't *blame* boots on the ground for not holding as much interest in a company's trajectory as upper management. Even tiers below the C-suite, like HR, generally only see changes to their day-to-day experience based on whether they have an employer dispensing timely checks (assuming that this is a healthy work environment — we *do not* want to be the CFOs who lurk and grumble all over the office because we fumbled a product launch)

The key to connecting non-C-suite employees with our mindsets is fuelling the perception that they are invested in our goals; and in reality, when you do well at employee engagement, this isn't so much of a perception as a fact.

So, to circle back to the main idea: *what is employee engagement?* To expand off our initial explanation, it is grounding employees on the role they play in the organization. Amplifying their excitement to fulfill said role.

Employees must be more than numbers. No matter how big or small an organization is, they must feel like meaningful, heard members of a powerful group because their ideas, presence, and contributions matter.

To instill this in the workforce, employees must understand the process and the people involved, as well as their functions. Once employees get a grasp of the mechanisms, they will gain an awareness of how they fit into the big picture. Productivity competitions and functions are great, but understanding the big pictures is how all members thrive and stay.

What is Morale?

...but that isn't all! Morale is another major piece in yielding the right result, and excluding it is like forgetting to multiply by the right function in an algebraic equation. Your calculations are going to be off, plus you're going to get an ugly red mark when the teacher passes it back.

No one wants to get the red pen.

To avert unfavorable outcomes, let's analyse what morale entails. **Morale** is the positive energy derived from being engaged. We're talking about the confidence and enthusiasm of a group at any time.

Heeding what we discussed about the overlap between C-suite and other departments' goals, you'd predict that a motivated workforce would be better able to produce desirable results. You can compare this to how *some* may manage to dig themselves out of a troubling situation, while others flounder despite possessing baseline resources; but when you contrast the overall outcomes of the two categories, you quickly learn that starting on an even footing is much more conducive to success than struggling.

Ideally, a C-suite executive wants their workers to find the challenge in surpassing expectations with the job, not checking the standard requirements. If the routine to-do list is inducing crippling migraines amongst your workforce, then it's time to assess whether there are outside factors at play that are hampering their performance.

If all is well in the work environment, decent amenities, provisions, and so on, then it's time to look at the excess rewards we're distributing to keep employees at their prime output. Just taking a quick glance at the apex of human competition, such as athletics or superstardom, an often-cited reason for winners to retire from their positions is a lack of challenges. No, these individuals have not spent so long training that they've evolved into superhumans, numb to the strain of pushing yourself every day (although we'd wager, they have a better tolerance for discomfort than the average couch potato). It still takes a lot out of a dancer to show up to the studio at a set time every morning, practice for hours on end so that they don't regress nor fall behind on new styles.

The gap in rewards versus effort, however, grows larger and larger the more you succeed. A top performer in the workplace is going to attain all the salary increases and security you can imagine. Reflect on your role, for example, as a C-suite executive, and contemplate all the times you've run into complacency now that you've beaten the grind. It isn't a cakewalk to be at the top of the ladder, no, but you aren't beholden to a strict regimen to surpass the thousands of people who are vying for a spot at the top. While you sit at the peak of a wobbly ladder, there's a mountain of bodies clawing at each other, desperate to ascend by even one rung. But even the rungs themselves are swarmed, too packed with iron-clenched fists to grab. So, you can't latch onto the sixtieth or fortieth place, you've got to keep climbing.

If you're dedicated, and doused with a pinch of luck, then you may ascend the breadth of competition one day. It'll be satisfying, it'll be all you've ever worked towards...and then there's nothing above to grasp onto.

This centers on the main issue with maintaining employee productivity. The average workplace does not exist to such extremes as the example provided, but the high performers do encounter the same tedium you see in winners elsewhere. Step outside of that bubble, and you'll see people with not a fraction of the resolve as these personalities, who'll also need a promise of gratification dangled ahead of them. After all, who wants to run a nonstop race? Humans need breaks, reminders that they'll be treated in the end (regardless of what "the end" might look like for your specific expectation), feedback that they're applying the right technique (if someone is on the off-road barefoot, it'd benefit for them to know earlier than when they're rocking to-and-fro on the picnic chair, clutching a swollen toe), and if their feedback on the conditions of the competition (if the race is hosted in the middle of the worst storm the town has seen yet, they'd better hear that you're aware of the change in circumstance and are ready to remedy your demands!) is reaching open ears.

Missing Pieces

If you're just coming to the bitter realization that your workforce is not, in fact, hopping in their bedroom when they learn that today is their turn to clock into work, don't fret. The most profitable of businesses invest thousands, if not millions, of dollars into initiatives that are focused on increasing employee engagement. You have probably gone through one of these yourself; the random seminar where you're suddenly asked to introduce your favorite anime and Zodiac sign to a team that you've hardly uttered a word to in the 12 years you've been at a company, or the "fitness" day where everyone is dragged outside to sweat up their work uniform before return to keyboard-clacking.

Yes, we all have sour memories of a businesses' means of "connecting with the team." Not nearly enough C-suite executives exploit the strategies that'll make their endeavors successful, because the methodology is a lot more complex than you think. It's no calculus conundrum, and we thank the heavens for it, but it's laborious enough that the less focused will shun proper research in favor of the effortless road. Also known as throwing nonsense at a wall until one sloppy projectile sticks.

A broken clock is right once a day, and maybe if you experiment with enough approaches, you'll find the most cost-effective way to bolster engagement without challenging yourself. But if you don't want to test your resources and sanity, it's best to embark on a conclusive path to results.

Where's the Engagement?

As you thrust forward into your company's newest seasonal objective, you gear up to prep your employees for the metrics they'll need to meet. Bigger ambitions don't necessarily correlate to bigger budgets, so I'd imagine that this makeover doesn't comprise a thickened roster, meaning there'll be a relatively similar number of heads under your leadership, but a widened set of expectations. Everyone will have to challenge themselves to merely gain purchase on these demands — exceeding them, which is the visceral pining of any C-suite executive whether they voice it aloud or not, is a whole different beast to overcome.

While you eagerly garnish your latest employee report with the strokes of your fancy fountain pen, the employees below are fixated on a different goal, one admittedly narrower than yours. And that goal is attaining their personal career expectations.

For a lot of professionals, well-paying job security is the bulk of their career expectations. Others hanker to summit the career ladder and join your exclusive C-club, but for most workers, getting by is the goal. People don't voluntarily show up to make someone else more money than themselves every day, so why wouldn't they conform to a looser set of expectations?

Your responsibility is to budge in and correct that line of thinking. Cementing a purpose for employees to strive for will engage them with the business's goals. But what will that purpose owe up to?

Values are unique to an individual. Some are voracious for success; others are prideful with humility. That's why fast-paced work environments attract such staggering turnover rates, despite striving to make up for the success in the form of hours and pay. For some personalities, financial gain simply isn't worth the level of exertion certain companies will hold you to. Others consider it their natural calling.

Between this contrast of desires and theme emerges chemistry. A company, its brand and mission must resonate with the people who play a part in propagating it. Imagine a billion-dollar company where the workers don't believe they'll scrape by single-digit sales. You'd think they were joking around or incredulous, because you'd have to associate yourself with a brand so powerful because you have faith in its eminence — that your job won't randomly be snatched up by the dice-roll of consumer disenchantment.

Lock in on your workers' purpose. They must be pivoted towards a grander ambition than meeting the bare minimum to collect their pay every other week. What goal is incredibly intimate to them, serving their better interests?

Better yet, what goals can you think of that have longevity? It is one thing to aspire to a temporary ideal, surpassing sales in one week, as you'd see in one of those competitions where salespeople are challenged to rival each other's commission, and a far more meaningful act to collectively pursue long-term change.

To ensure your company's growth, you want to inspire a mentality shift that sticks with the culture. When your workforce is driven towards raising the bar on a rotating basis, then new hires won't have to be re-educated on the importance of striving beyond their comfort. The example will be modeled for them, thus creating a result that is permanent.

A lot of business leaders don't think to launch campaigns that are rooted in the long term, because they don't see their employees as assets to chisel overtime. This may come as a surprise, as it's intuitive that talents who you retain for an extended period provide more value than enduring the process of scouting and training new professionals. When your business operates at a small capacity, the line of communication between the topmost levels and the boots on the ground becomes a lot more seamless, so it's easier to transfer goals between the two.

As a company expands, however, you'll need to establish a lot of intermediaries to enforce and take feedback. The CFO isn't reviewing every single complaint submitted by the workers on the ground floor. That'd not only be unrealistic, but a waste of business resources. "Mediums" must be placed between the various levels of an organization to ensure that those in prominent roles invest their energy in tasks that require their unique attention.

Simultaneously, C-suite executives mustn't see their "middle management" figures as stand-in mail pigeons to ferry all discourse between polar opposite levels in a business. C-suite executives remain the most responsible for ensuring that a response is given. Whether that culminates in changes to the workplace, or rearrangements in the company's internal structure. Your subordinates don't have unbridled power to shake up every element of the business' practices, so you must be vigilant in maintaining a "presence" that stays attuned to the general sentiments.

Impediments

Employee engagement, the coveted achievement it is, is perfected by few companies. With all the promise it holds, you'd believe it'd thrive at a much higher rate than it does. Yet there are so many impediments that prevent C-suite executives from letting it flourish.

Time is the enemy of many ambitions. There is an old saying, the best time to plant a tree was 10 years ago — the second-best time is *now*. Indeed, if you've turned to this book, you've likely observed the consequences of business practices you've failed to vet or implement. Some issues are remedied through quick fixes, especially if your operations exist at a small level. There likely wasn't much of an audience to bristle, and if you polish your reputation, you can expand your reach to a widened demographic who won't be familiar with your early failures.

Yet, everyone is lucky to dust themselves off without so little as a scratch. A lot of brands stain their reputations, lose their footing in the talent recruitment market, strain their trust with customers due to a string of poor habits. While we can vocalize the importance of allowing forgiveness and growth, *no one is entitled to someone else's money*. As a financial entity, your relationship with consumers and employees is dependent on material delivery. You must meet your promise on the services, the products you advertise to customers. If the quality does not meet the standards you claim, they have every right to withhold their money for future deliverables. Same goes for employees who'll exit the business if they find the business to fall below the expectations they had in mind.

An ineptly trained workforce will have lost a lot of time in the productivity department. They'll have missed sales goals, possibly soured a lot of customers (repeat and potential), and limited their own potential to improve upon weaknesses. Like an infected wound, the longer you leave internal business problems to fester, the gnarlier they'll become. It's much easier to slay a small foe than a large beast, so most companies neglect strain between upper management and their subordinates, as the upfront cost to address the problem is so daunting.

It is not as if ignoring a problem will make it go away. If you skip out on a doctor's appointment because you think their diagnosis will take away time from work, the concern you had likely won't just magically disappear — it'll worsen, and the complications of it will stratify, too. You can pretend like it's an offense on your schedule to book out 30 minutes in the day to identify the root cause or dig your head in the sand and see how that "minor ache" grows into a debilitating condition that puts you out of work permanently.

Business must run efficiently, and it's no easy task deciding where to divest resources in order to see the biggest returns. Understandably, a C-suite executive freshly instated at a company would be reluctant to handle problems that have mounted up on the to-do pile for years. The possibility of intermediate failures is high, and the trajectory to success is long.

Ultimately, this does not negate the importance of correcting issues while it is still possible to do so. A temporary obstruction can quickly become a chronic burden. Circling back to the quote about planting trees, we know that it relates to the essential nature of plants on our Earth. While we can't reverse the damage we've done to our planet all these centuries, we can preserve the "unstable" remnants of what we have by aggressively moving towards an eco-friendly future.

When you first approach a heap of issues, it may seem impossible to ever trudge to the end of the pile. Since a lot of C-suite executives are driven to prove themselves to be the most capable, they'd naturally be averse to absorbing serious risks like ploughing hours towards a solution.

Nevertheless, you've been granted your role because you're expected to analyse risk versus cost, leading your team to a resolution that maximises future rewards. If a much-needed resolution demands your team's utmost efforts, and will take weeks, if not months to achieve, you must weigh the cost of letting it be, if not addressing it passively.

Your subordinates are not the only one being assessed for their contributions to the business. Your decision-making as a leader will determine whether you're the right fit for the company's success. Perhaps a smaller business may not hold authority votes when periods get tough, but once shareholders join the mix, you can't expect to laze out on responsibilities and keep your power.

Time is one of the scarcest, desired resources. Everyone wishes they could've chosen the right road earlier, could've done something when they were at the peak of their capabilities

— but regardless of whether your business is in peak form or not, it's imperative that you grasp your fleeting security in the market and fight to retain the fragile consumer faith you have. Do the work to engage your employees, because when a major scandal unfolds due to their lackadaisical efforts, it will be you who shoulders the blame.

Resources are another impediment to fostering engagement. Notwithstanding the efficiency any sensible business must run on, shoestring budgets are pervasive, and many businesses are left with little after they pay salaries. When you are in the stage of growing your brand, the focus must be set on reinvesting what you earn in funding improvements and expansion measures. For a typical business, this may look like hiring more talent or upgrading product aesthetics. Whichever the case, employee desires often come last. There is a strong mentality in the industry that fledgling workers must "struggle it out" until the business flourishes, and only then can they see noticeable improvements to their quality of work experience.

While this may be logical to those at the top of management, who clock into far more extravagant facilities than the average subordinate (you may be inclined to pat yourself on the back for building up the business while subsisting on rice and beans, but don't lie that you haven't got an ergonomic chair and two-tier desk in your office), your employees will essentially be "iced out" from seeing the impact of their daily contributions. If they feel like inessential members of the team, it's no wonder they won't feel invested in the company's success. What does it matter when sales goals are surpassed, when the communal bathroom still stinks like the local zoo?

Reinvesting your profits into growing the company must also mean divesting some money to the side for employees.

Treat them with collaborative functions, initiatives meant to platform their voices. Above all, ensure you have the manpower necessary to be reactive to their feedback. There is nothing more isolating than a company that demands every inch of energy you're worth yet can't get back to a simple complaint that has been filed weeks ago. In every instance that you take in a new batch of employees, you must make sure that you have the resources prepared to support their trajectories for success. Expecting everyone to just "figure it out" on a whim or strain themselves to make up for support you've failed to provide will only attract some of the lowest quality employees to your team. Talents who know their worth and want to associate with a brand that'll enhance their skills won't go somewhere that'll drain them more than they do help them.

Education is another factor that impacts employee engagement. A lot of managers aren't made aware of how their decisions alienate employees. Many are used to the traditional corporate culture of respondents heeding everything their bosses say simply because they said so. While this may have worked in the past when the concept of respect was heavily upheld, a lot of businesses are struggling to resonate with younger generations that are a lot more questioning of authority. They aren't going to jump to follow your orders just because you wave a title; they've seen the consequences of hazardous workplaces, how lives have been harmed because employees blindly followed their leaders.

I'd hope that your business does not languish at such a low level where such complaints are voiced; thanks to government initiatives, businesses are forced to implement a certain standard of employee protections so that they aren't severely compromising their wellbeing on the job. Reducing hazards must not be a concern as you turn to this book, but rather mending the issue of motivating an increasingly labor-jaded workforce. Perhaps workers have never been joyous over the prospect of working for someone else, but there's no denying that the lengths to which they were willing to put their personal desires aside for the greater good of the company used to be a lot bigger.

Nowadays, it is not uncommon for workers to either apply for a job simply because it is the best way to sustain their own lifestyle, or because they had no other choice. These sorts of personalities aren't connected to your brand's mission; they're present to serve one sole purpose, and that is their personal interests.

Thus, you can't assume that your demands will be met simply because your subordinates are obligated to fulfill them. You must grasp the cultural shift that fuels a lot of indifferent emotions towards leaders and go the extra mile to make all your employees feel like they're on relatively equal footing.

"That's crazy!" you're probably thinking, citing the years you've worked up to your own prestigious title in the C-suite. It seems ludicrous that a new, junior employee would demand that they be treated just like a professional who has remained loyal to the company for years. And I'd agree, there must be divisions kept between the responsibilities and privileges assigned to the two groups. At the same time, they are both entitled to a level of respect that, once breached, must be understood to bring professional consequences.

Lack of Empowerment Within the Culture

Humans are complex creatures. As swiftly as we can feel like we've been propelled to echelons of capability, we can plummet to the debts of insecurity.

Insecurity can manifest in many forms. Some doubt their personal self-worth, whether their level of inner pride is in line with where they actually stand relative to others within their community. Within a workplace, this sense of self-esteem would be centered on their jobs. Different roles dispense different expectations and outcomes. While we're normally educated on the potential for career growth when we're introduced to a new place of employment, some environments breed more opportunities than others.

This disparity in future opportunities can make some employees feel classed out. A motivated individual is a person who possesses full autonomy over their actions. They're someone whose position matters, whose identity complements their wider surroundings.

A lot of companies fall short on the empowerment front. They strip employees of their personal sense of direction and question why there's declined productivity as employees integrate into the environment. If you recruit dozens of talents every season and continually encounter issues with keeping employees at their best behavior, then perhaps the issue isn't the job market. Perhaps the issue is your leadership.

Employees are members of a community. A thriving community must encourage its members to learn of each other's unique traits, to interact and be heard. Contrast the material success of communities where inhabitants are open to embracing diverse beliefs and service multiple needs, versus townships that haven't evolved since the toilet was invented. Sounds like an exaggeration, and hopefully there aren't spaces where beliefs have lagged that much behind others. The point is that when you analyse scientific developments, quality of life and rates of achievements in these two different communities, the progressive counterparts always stride ahead in success.

For as much as we cling onto tradition and "keeping simple as is," the reality is that inclusivity lays the groundwork for growth, and growth is the only way to grasp success. You can't stagnate and expect to stay on top of your field. That's why top athletes retire after they recognize they're unable to commit to the same rigorous regimens as they used to, on top of adopting modernized techniques that'll place them with younger talents.

A lot of businesses like to fancy themselves the trailblazer that has absolutely disrupted the market. And I think that we can name a couple of brands that, in the past couple of decades, swept into the public eye and completely changed our purchasing habits: DVD rentals switching to streaming, for example, and the proliferation of mobile devices. Who would've thought that humans would be carrying minicomputers in the early 20th century?

These innovations, groundbreaking as they are, are not only exceedingly rare, but swiftly replicated. After all, take a quick glance at the marketplace and watch the mass of results that crop up for sleek portable devices. Apple stands as a global leader alongside brands like Samsung, and even newer competitors like Google and Huawei.

Search for lower priced alternatives, and you'll glimpse companies that you've never seen uttered in an everyday conversation. Yet you can bet that these brands have raked in millions for supplying a market that has been neglected by these behemoth, ever-bloating brands.

This is all to say that markets aren't static, nor are companies (allowed to be). If Apple decides one day that their approach to maximise profits is closing in on the affordable market, then they'll have to take their lower-priced competitors more seriously. Otherwise, they'll fall behind and plummet to the bottom of the race. We've seen the ruins of empires who assumed they were too big to fall (Blockbuster, Circuit City) and now disintegrate in abandoned areas.

A forward-thinking C-suite executive must propel their team for constant growth. That involves reshaping their approach to leadership and employee empowerment as the company evolves. A new crop of employees might not be responsive to the methods you used to integrate employees when you started. To go even further, some brands lack an internal branding strategy to begin with. This serious gap muddles a business's identity and pronounces the division between upper management and the boots on the ground.

Your engagement strategy must be woven into the fabric of an organization, not a singular person. It must catalyze a movement, a way of being amongst the workforces. By connecting everyone to the cause, you emphasize their interest in sustaining the brand's success.

Financial Impacts

Weighing the costs of implementing new procedures in the workplace, C-suite executives are prone to raise one question: what do we lose financially by skimping out on it?

Ideally, no business goes out of their way to neglect improvements if they have the resources to do so comfortably. Debates take place on resource expenditure *because* you have to strain the company to see improvement. Ironically, running a business tends to mirror what it's like to train the human body. Honing your muscles takes constant exertion, which correlates to willingly placing yourself in a position of discomfort. If it was easy to get a six-pack, everyone would haul themselves to the gym on a routine basis to thrash those reps.

Fitness holds prestige because we know that it's hard. Exercise, even as you continually expose yourself to physical challenges day after day, tests you in both the body and the mind. It probably won't anguish you to do 200 push-ups on month six compared to day 1, but it won't be as intuitive as pressing a staple into sheets of paper. Everything that yields high returns requires high dedication.

Yet, in an industry where shoestring budgets and meaningless one-track decision-making prevails, it's not surprising to see employment engagement get neglected. Given the multitude of aspects you must oversee as you grow a business, you're constantly juggling one task after another, accelerating into a new project once you've barely submitted a prior accomplishment.

There is no room to slow down in the business world. If you ever feel like the entire company has earned a long break, then something has gone wrong. Your company is edging the fall. This isn't to say that breaks must be shunned, but no matter the time or place, there must always be a project running in the background: a next goal, a reassessed standard.

For those who have underscored the importance of employee engagement, they're destined to see the repercussions as time goes on. If you're referencing this book as you endure the lows, you might recognize these impacts: absenteeism, turnovers, loss of productivity, lack of loyalty.

$$\mathit{Absenteeism\ Rate} =$$

$$\left(\frac{\mathit{Total\ Number\ of\ Days\ Employees\ were\ Absent}}{\mathit{Total\ Workdays\ Available\ in\ a\ Fixed\ Period}}\right) \times 100$$

Tardiness is a sore spot for a lot of organizations. To add what we mentioned earlier about shifting attitudes amongst younger generations in the workforce, attendance is becoming a growing problem with younger talents. Their mentality surrounding the work environment is heavily dimmed by the belief that they're "in it for the paycheck," which, doubtless, we acknowledge that employees' contributions are fixed to monetary returns. If a business' returns for retaining a specific employee does not outweigh what they bring, then they'll be let go. It's not like you're learning everyone's personality traits and inviting them over for dinner. Work is a strictly professional environment, although some may justify presenting the bare minimum because they resent that dynamic.

You may ask, how is anyone supposed to make an employee feel like their purpose is bigger than the position they're tied to? After all, your relationship with a worker starts and ends with the business. You likely wouldn't know them outside of it; and if you do, it's not encouraged that you allow intimate biases to interfere with your judgement of their performance.

The answer lies in maintaining professional boundaries while reinforcing the value your company provides relative to competitors. Even for the jaded job hunters, every professional knows there are work environments that are heavenly to deal with compared to others. Most personalities, for example, wouldn't willingly seek out a high-stress job. They simply cope with it due to the financial compensation.

As employee's demands grow in the workforce, you can't expect to have your cake and eat it too. Concessions will need to be made to reap the same advantages businesses used to when they took on new talent. Job seekers are a lot more discerning with what brands they choose to affiliate with, so you're already pulling from a tough selection when you're establishing your name in the industry. On the positive side, workers' interest with favoring positive employee cultures over traditional benefits lends smaller businesses a chance to prove themselves due to broadened outlooks. People are no longer flocking to the same few companies and looking down on the rest. Many professionals who could get hired at highly competitive businesses if they tried, are opting for smaller, intimate environments where they know their personal needs will be met. Look at the number of workers who leave Google or Tesla. These brands are amongst the most coveted in the world, but reputation alone can't compensate for being reduced to a number for the rest of your professional life.

Lack of Transparency

We imbalance the power between roles in an organization so that ideally, pivotal decisions lie in the hands of the most qualified people. You aren't going to have a new hire negotiate a seven-figure brand deal or invite every single member of the company to your shareholder meetings. Decisions made at the top level of a business trickle down to employees that exist below, but everyone must focus their efforts on different areas. That is how a business thrives — by putting talents towards where they're most useful.

Some businesses take this practice to efficiently designate tasks. Others, I'd imagine many of which the leaders are referencing this book, default to this dynamic to excuse poor communication.

Boots on the ground respond to their managers, but that does not mean that they are powerless or less significant than the former. Analyse the whole picture of the business, and you'll see that the collective actions taken by boots on the ground inform the impact they have on their target audience. This is why the makeup at the lower levels of an organization is a lot more volatile than the highest rungs. You want to maintain a certain quality of performance to enhance your impression on the market. C-suite executives can't just slack off and expect for the company to continue to grow, but it'd be a lot more detrimental if even a fraction of the boots on the ground decided to skip work for a week than the CFO.

As you can see, people who lie at polar-opposite ends of an organization are heavily dependent on one another. Employees, they look to the apex of management for meaningful change — there's no use for middle management if they absorb feedback like a sponge, enacting zero improvements in response to the complaints they receive. The only people in the position to switch out and empower "softer" authority are the people who oversee them, and so it is up to C-suite executives to communicate effectively with their employees.

Alas, employee engagement is frequently stifled by transparency issues. You'll see businesses where the team is no bigger than a dozen, yet the topmost leader is borderline unreachable as a worker or contractor. Frustrating as it is as a worker who might want to report flaws with the workplace's facilities or policies, imagine being on the ground with a customer, unable to relay their concerns because the boss is cut off from the rest of the organization. Sure, it's not as if your average big box store is structured to field complaints to the CFO; there are supervisors on the ground level present to not only coach you on the accepted practice but react to the way you approach your obligations.

Yet, there will be instances where a salesperson runs into an especially difficult transaction. Perhaps a customer wants to make an exchange that goes against the company policy. Or a customer requests a return after identifying a fault with the product's manufacturing.

Unless you have only patronized the most pristine shopping centers on the planet, you've probably witnessed firsthand what a "blindly follow corporate" sales floor looks like, and it's far from appealing. A lack of flexibility in return policies, poorly designed store layouts, and a lack of consideration for the community that is being targeted are telltale signs of this deficit. It isn't as if the local manager hasn't made notice of the inconveniences you observe. They're not clocking in, happy to take a dozen complaints about their poorly organized store.

Ultimately, an upper management that is severely divorced from the day-to-day transpirations of those who serve them will cause these mishaps. Rather than feed the chaos, you must pause and deliberate, as a C-suite executive, if you've done enough to heed the feedback of those who work under you. No, drafting a quick questionnaire for yourself to answer won't suffice; the truth will only come from those who are directly affected, and that relies on strengthening the communication line between you and the various levels of your company's organization.

The old heads at your job will probably side-eye you at first, bewildered that you're extending yourself to an outside group. "Don't you know there are people hired to handle that for you?" is a predictable jibe if not, "We can't enable the employees to become overly dependent on us. They must learn to solve problems for themselves."

Isolated from the issue, these are all valid remarks. A leader in charge of an efficient business mustn't "hand hold" their workers until they grasp the right process. Talents must be recruited based on their ability to adapt and present apt ability;

after that, they must understand how to best-manage situations regardless of whether there is authority present to resolve the situation.

But even if you search for the perfect employee and pen a perfect set of guidelines to follow, there are bound to be deviations on the ground when you invite unpredictable factors like customer interaction and the dice-roll of a non-laboratory environment. When you are setting standards for your workforce, it's important to remember that life isn't a replica of polished facts and conclusions. Human behavior tends to err from a straight line, and that deviation will have your employees react in different ways to your expectations.

In all, keep an accessible, clear process in place for employees to relay their opinions to authority in your organization. Once they're able to witness that their voices are being acknowledged, there'll be a shift in the connection they feel towards their job.

Lack of Value for the Asset, the Employee

Your employees are not interchangeable pieces of property. I know that we commonly reference the workforce in terms of signifying "value" and "output," but we must acknowledge that there are humans behind these contributions. Humans have needs, emotions, and reactions.

The stagnant corporate environment is one where workers are hustled in, negligent of their wellbeing, then deluged with responsibilities to finish before a predetermined deadline. Think of the harsh conditions in factories, retail environments with high turnover and even numerous fast-food establishments. For the popular stores that manage to get away with this culture, there has been growing backlash over the years to their policies and internal evolutions in how they benefit employees. McDonalds, for example, isn't the ideal workplace for those who want to lounge and labor at their own pace; however, there are multiple "lifelines" in place to bolster employees when they feel like they're overwhelmed. Some franchises offer healthcare benefits, others show how they go above governmental safety regulations to ensure the health of their workers. You may not be promised a heaping pay for taking on the job, but you can expect your managers to commit to a level of professionalism that doesn't exist at your local mom-and-pop.

Even retail environments have become increasingly fluid in response to employees' grievances. The brands that failed to evolve with the desires of the workforce have failed to survive. Big-box stores like Sears faced a sharp decline in eminence this century. Noting that your boots on the ground generally overlap with the personnel who interact most with consumers — thus absorb the bulk of their feedback — it is pertinent that you treat their perspectives with respect. They may provide commentary on issues you'd be oblivious to high up on your corporate ladder, considering how disparate the resonance between audience demands and business actions seems to be nowadays.

Lack of Direction and Expectation

Don't throw your employees to the wolves. There's no quicker way to kill someone's motivation for a project's longevity than a lack of focus. Businesses are essentially large, multi-step projects, so when you introduce new workers to your team, you must grasp that they are looking to partake in a coherent vision.

Business leaders tend to possess a lot of confidence, as you don't veto high-risk moves on a routine basis when you lack faith in your abilities. Amongst your peers in the C-suite, you probably don't need to look far to see a hint of ego; and this is no sour point, as strong-willed people are prepped to butt heads and challenge systems in order for positive change. It is important to assess, considering this prevalent personality type, whether you're assigning a lot of value to the input that arises outside of your bubble.

Passing down a detailed list of rules to follow isn't enough to lead your team to success. Even with intermediary managers working to message your ambitions to the lower levels, companies can mimic "broken telephone" when there are so many mouths to pass through and a thick wall between the person calling the shots and the people making those requests happen.

Your priority as a C-suite executive must be fine-tuning your strategy to your workforces' rates of success. Are they responding well to the orders you handed out? If the answer is no, it may be time to question whether you've missed some holes in your strategy. Perhaps the discrepancy boils down to poor communication, or maybe the plan itself is misaligned with reality. With a vigilant mindset, you must be able to stay on top of collecting these observations as feedback, thereafter, capitalizing on the knowledge to produce an efficient resolution.

Keep in mind throughout this process that it is *alright* to make mistakes as a C-suite executive. If you've been working at a company for more than a day and haven't recorded one personal mishap, you're either playing ignorant or deliberately blocking yourself from criticism.

Workers are human, from the boots on the ground to upper management. We anticipate a level of perfection in the workplace, but performance can never reach the 100% mark. There will be dips, oversights, and even novice accidents. It can seem crazy, being a professional for so long and yet slipping up as a beginner would, but practice only familiarizes you with the choices to take. It doesn't shield you from mistakes.

Not to mention, mistakes only equate to failure when they aren't properly addressed. If you haven't learned from the missteps you take, you're bound to repeat them again — quote that "those who leave the pasta in the microwave are doomed to reheat it twice" — so heed the flaws in your leadership so you can better hold a position of command. Regardless of whether your colleagues are as receptive to their own weaknesses, you have a personal responsibility to yourself as a professional, and those who serve you in a company, to apply the best discernment possible when you enter the workplace. So, allow a bit of leeway to use work as a training ground if it'll foster improved management. Employees need the honed leadership.

Ineffective Chain of Communication

Remember when we talked about the detriment a bloated employee roster can be to a company's growth? The HR in a business must be skillfully led towards hiring practices that prioritize honing complimentary talents over recycling batches of professionals who stay for a short period. A company that prizes longevity will reflect that in its internal structure, because it's difficult to retain a high standard of culture when the people who comprise it are constantly revolving.

Productivity isn't the only part of a business's output that gets hampered by employee bloat. The chain of communication *depends* on leadership being in clear contact with one another, and that relies on them being able to effectively relay messages to those above and below them. Internal leadership that struggles to properly direct the workforce will end up sabotaging decisions that must be made. You'll run into instances where hard choices meet a deadlock in upper management but imagine the burden of that multiplied by a thousand when the people who respond to you can't keep your workforce in order.

As of late, too many employees of major companies — brands who, we, the public, assumed to be infallible, flawless in their handling of internal matters — decry their bosses' failure to address reports that detail criminal concerns they suffered from or witnessed. While you can go and brush off any form of feedback as a "petty complaint," amidst the minor criticisms can be a severe concern that is swept under the rug with the so-called sludge.

On top of that, workers will become reluctant to voice concerns if they fear pushback, never mind a lack of responsiveness. When you, someone who holds one of the positions with the most power in a company, don't show an urgency to heed the voices of those who serve you, there's a chance that your smaller authority will abuse their ranks knowing that there will be no repercussions. So long as they are the last in line to hear the boots on the ground's concerns, who is going to correct them?

To reference an intensive job, I once coached a corporation. One of my first recommendations was to improve organizational communication. I recognized that despite the company's flourishing revenue, internal weaknesses hurt the potential profit they could squeeze out of an efficient structure. Following my advice, the company hired a team member who specifically oversees staff communication. A weekly newsletter was also put in place, occurring alongside increased meetings and small training sessions.

Basic Dysfunction

We hate to predetermine the capabilities of someone based on their background, because no one likes to be written off, and it's unhealthy to live based on preconceptions. Nonetheless, a C-suite executive holds a huge responsibility to act from experience to make informed judgements. Without putting your team in a position to fail, you'll have to, in select situations, act based upon patterns. Existing research, red flags and the like cannot only drive essential decisions; they can tell you which candidates are not fit for your environment.

As we've mentioned the downside of assessing employees merely on their credentials, we must consider that not all professionals start on an equal footing. Some are just entering the workforce when they apply for a position in your company, while others have had extensive experience working under someone else's command.

Despite the obvious advantages of hiring someone with related industry cosigns, it's essential that we realize that not all experiences are equal. Yes, a recommendation from an authority within another company can signify that someone stood out in a professional space, but the capabilities that caused them to shine elsewhere might not translate well under your leadership.

Matter of fact, the disparity in professionalism between different brands can be so large that their experience may serve as more of a detriment than a positive. Not all employees are trained to operate efficiently. The existence of this book proves that a lot of C-suite executives flounder to grasp the challenge of properly leading their workforce. And while it's a tough task to ask of any professional, the fact that so many employees languish under poor instruction breeds a group of professionals who don't possess the right mindset. They could've been forced to put up with a culture that emanates low morale, or that buckled under dysfunction. They could've never seen a line of management that leads their subordinates appropriately.

That being considered, you must practice patience when implementing the steps to bolster employee engagement. People aren't going to be equally receptive to these improvements when you first introduce them. Certain personalities, sadly, might not be able to uphold a healthy and productive work culture definitively.

Opportunities

Engagement Must Be the Pivotal Point

By this point in the book, you've received a lot of homework to improve your company. I know, I know, an extra lesson might seem like a way to overflow the crippling load, but these tips will all benefit you in the end. And of all the information provided, you must prioritize making *this* happen.

Without engaged employees, your ambitions will never align with the performance of your workforce. Think of it like trying to prepare a complex recipe, and you have all the ingredients and tools that you need but follow the instructions in the wrong order.

The resulting dish won't lend the same flavors, if it even matches the aesthetics you desire to create. Baking, especially, requires that you mix ingredients at the right pace and order. Look at the difference between brownies that mix the wet and dry ingredients beforehand, versus the ones that randomly incorporate them in the pre-baked mixture. It's evident that the steps you take to approach a desired outcome cannot be dismissed, and for a financial entity with multiple jobs and dollars on the line, you don't want to neglect the essentials that build a strong company's foundation.

Make engagement weave the fabric of the company together. To take it a step further, uphold it as the essential material that forms your internal culture. Your brand's public mission must reflect in the way you connect employees to your private goals. Maintain a consistent vision, and you'll see that employees adapt to delivering consistent results when they enter the workplace. Employees mustn't be subject to conflicting, isolating treatment simply for the fact that they contribute to your businesses' growth behind closed doors, shielded from the public's scrutiny.

Mission, Vision, and Values

It's never too late to return to the basics and whip up what you've neglected to institute in the beginning. Unless your company is still in the formative stages, in which case now is a better time than ever, but outline the culture you need based on the unique values of your workforce.

Three reactive factors must shape your company's internal culture. The first is the reception of your sales audience. It might sound strange considering they don't have an intimate look into the structure of your business, but their interactions with the boots on the ground and other visible employees must inform how you train them prior to sending them out.

The second would be the perspectives of those in authority. That'd encompass you in the C-suite, among the workers who lay the groundwork for goals that'll propel the company forward.

The third, and perhaps most important, class must be your subordinates. That includes the feedback from HR, the concerns voiced by employees at different levels of the organization, and the observations you take on their progressive performance. Studying their ease at integrating into the work environment, it is your obligation to tweak and protect the qualities to best serve those who you ask the most out of.

Constant Reminders of What is Expected

Your workers aren't psychic, and no matter how clear you might find your instruction to be, humans are variable in how they interpret and act upon demands.

A company that is adaptive to the market will be flush with diverse personalities, and those differing perspectives serve as an asset when improperly utilized. However, they can fuel disorganization and air a lack of focused identity.

You must never assume that what you ask of your workers is a clear-cut obligation. Follow them through the process through the feedback of middle management, checking to ensure that they're meeting projections in terms of intermediary deadlines. If performance falls below expectations, it's your job to analyse what could've fueled that failure. Was the approach you recommended inept? Are employees resonating with the goals you assign? Be diligent and get to the crux of the issue urgently.

Constant Reminders of Acceptable Culture

Once you establish an ideal image of what the workplace must look like, connect to employees to uphold that concept. Basically, upgrade that "vision" to a reality!

Even adults can mirror the faults of toddlers at times. Showing someone the ropes once isn't enough to instill a permanent mindset. You must remain with them throughout the slip ups, the accidents, and the moments they forget your teachings altogether. If you're using HR's resources efficiently, you won't assign them to head the most thorough training program that lasts for months on end. They'll have to "release" employees to the wild that is practical job experience eventually, and that means there is no hand-holding or constant leadership hovering over your team.

Through their increased independence, remind employees that there is a structure to follow and that you are there to ensure their success. When they are aware that standards are being routinely vetted, they'll have an incentive to sustain positive habits.

Be Enthusiastic to Invest Money in Your People

Show your employees they're valued with monetary rewards! After years of toiling to reach the echelon of corporate achievement, it's natural to want to clutch your pennies and have subordinates work to see the same privileges. But the average employee isn't demanding to assume the CFO's role simply because they disagree with their leadership. A lot of workers simply desire to get by, and if they aren't 100% on board with how you choose to manage the business, it'd be a lot easier to swallow the bitterness with a nice compensation.

Treat your employees from time to time. The proof is in the pudding; when employees visually encounter the riches of their contributions, they'll grasp the upside to challenging themselves to attain higher productive output day after day.

KEY TAKEAWAYS

Leadership is a complicated responsibility, more so when you oversee delegating roles to countless people. Nevertheless, you can't see a little gain without mustering a little pain (okay, will admit this reads a little *too* cheesy), and propelling your team to greater heights will require you to operate outside of your comfort zone.

To efficiently manage employees, you must resonate with the general sentiments. And that requires engaging them and involving them in the trajectory of success, so that they feel like more than a number, and rather an essential piece in solving the equation.

Improvement is a studious, extensive journey. But when you connect your team with taking the right steps to approach a goal, reaching the endpoint becomes a lot easier.

Succession Planning

We've explored many challenges C-suite executives encounter managing employees. Optimizing a workforce, as you've learned, isn't limited to the pre-selection process as it extends to the efficacy of your training as the tools you use to prime your employees for success. Most professionals wish they could pull it off with the least amount of effort possible, but reality doesn't work out that way, especially not when you're at the top of the corporate ladder. Every accomplishment, every failure, will reflect on you (just look at those stock fluctuations), so it is in your best interest to not whoosh into bankruptcy territory.

This book has touched on quite a few topics; naturally, it might take a couple of rereads to soak all the lessons in. In fact, that's the best approach to any informational book. I think we can all recall a motivational book that we've stacked on our shelves as decorations rather than references. The first leaf-through always supplies a dopamine rush, where you'll feel like you're on top of the world after accessing the wealth of knowledge.

And then, one day will pass. Maybe you incorporate a few tidbits into your routine, haggle a colleague or two about how "life-changing" the author was.

Then, a week. By this point, 4AM mornings have fallen to the wayside. You promise yourself you'll commit to the gym, but that routine you drafted at the onset of the week has started to become shorter and shorter. And it's not because you've accomplished most of your goals — no, you haven't even broached the halfway milestone with them.

The issue lies in idealizing performance versus sustaining it. There's a pertinent saying: talk is easy, action is hard. A lot of people consume productivity tips like fast food, not meaningfully adopting the values they champion. When it comes to this book, it's important that you look at the main ideas as goals to be set instead of bookmarks to be met. Don't flip through the chapters without allowing the lessons to really sink in. There's a lot to digest here, so don't rush.

We've covered a lot of areas so far. It seems earned that we transition to a concept that interlinks all these ideas together. We've analysed hiring, managing, and assessing. Those are pretty broad focusses; however, they share a strong connection together, enhancing the use of employees.

Promotions can be viewed as the endgame of a worker's journey, if to use dramatic terms; as they progress to a better understanding of the company's needs, their value increases. Consequently, the business would want to expand the control they have over internal affairs; this is where promotions happen, and responsibilities surge.

There is an obvious incentive to empowering workers who've remained with your brand for a long period. You want to retain talent, so employees are generally handed raises in priority of experience and *capabilities*. Upgrading the authority of someone who is unproductive would be counterproductive to a company; similarly, thrusting someone into a strenuous position can scare them off if they're barely accustomed to the fringes. Promotions are an exercise of watchfulness and patience.

Not to mention, career mobility isn't a desirable trait for all. Your best worker will be diverse in personality qualities. Some will desire to lead teams, while others prefer to initiate by themselves. Think of independent successes versus team successes. Both are valuable in their own right, but placing someone in the wrong category can produce dismal results.

That introduces us to the importance of succession planning. Businesses may be founded by a single individual, but big ambitions take big investments. Not only will you have to seek a surplus of funds, but continually work to expand your employee roster based on output and innovation.

Succession breathes purpose into a cycle that otherwise airs, "hire, train, then repeat with the new batch." If the early segments of this book are still fresh in your mind, you're probably thinking, "Hey, I already know that I must avoid high employee turnover!" Retaining the talent, you dedicate resources to help shape a healthy business, but it isn't the entire framework. You must line up your assets for your company's expansion, and that involves succession planning.

Issues

Succession planning can appear deceptively simple. Every innovation runs its course. Whether it's a promising product launch, a pioneering campaign, or a new addition to the C-suite, your business will constantly need to shift its approach to see growth. That does not mean that internal shakeups must occur every moon cycle. You'll want to preserve what has proven effective for your organization.

That being said, there's always room to improve. In many instances, the best action would be to replace the leadership in a company structure. Instead of hemorrhaging the authorities you have in place, move the pieces around so that they work to their strengths.

Succession planning is a lot more valuable than it is given credit for. A lot of managers erroneously believe that they're paying their workers a favor by promoting them within the company. Let us preface this section by saying that promotions must be as beneficial to you as they are to your subordinates' salaries. If a company is interested in driving themselves towards longevity and growth, then they must constantly be on the lookout for talents who'll help fortify their mission.

The professionals you uplift play an important part in molding your brand's image. Promotions don't start and end with a fattened paycheck. You'll be serving an extended process of honing, vetting the right candidates for the position. The length and resources it takes to create a leader is often underestimated.

Succession Planning Synergizes All Elements of Business Management

When you explore this book, you'll discover that a company's health severely depends on the way it is managed. It is only consequential, then, that the people you place in charge reflect on the outcomes of your strategies. If your leadership is already in a state of disarray, you can't expect them to nominate subordinates who show desirable qualities. On the other hand, if you have a rigid band of authorities, with no plan in sight to invite new voices, then it's only inevitable that you'll run into stagnancy.

It's important to understand that your target audience is endlessly evolving. New generations will present new needs, and expanded focuses will present varying challenges to stay on top of the market.

It'd be arrogant to assume that you can cling onto the same set of authorities until the end of times, and still produce the same profits, let alone multiply them. The business industry is rife with competition, meaning there are tons of initiatives propelled by visionaries with double the resources and ambition. You can't afford to lag behind because of "tradition," "comfort," or "it always used to work this way."

When you view entrepreneurship as a bloated marketplace, it becomes clear why certain businesses buoy while others sink. You'll have businesses that bite the price of being "annoying" to push their products, doing everything they can to get their brand in others' faces. Then, you have the vendors that are content shuffling in the corner, believing that customers must gravitate towards them based on service quality alone.

Obviously, every consumer must appreciate a well-maintained brand. The problem is, there are so many companies saturating the market today, many of which are backed by big benefactors with access to the best connections and facilities possible. Can you really revolve your USP around your products alone when there are scores of others delivering the same, if not better?

Accepting that you're not one of a kind is always a sour feeling. No one likes to feel like they're a part of the masses, although we all scream our hearts out to tunes about wishing we could fit in and "blend in with the norms." The reality is, if you've thought of something, there is a high likelihood that someone has considered the same concept before. Look at how many derivations of the Rubix cube emerged around the same period before one scientist patented the design. Eventually, their copyright expired, and hundreds of competitors seized the marketplace, correcting the neglected flaws the creator failed to address in their product.

Note that we're speaking of one of the most iconic products in the world here. Imagine how that proliferates amongst less recognizable brands, particularly in niches that are just penetrating the marketplace. You need to sell your worth as aggressively as possible, but there is going to be a ton of resistance. People have heard of the next big thing since the dawn of time. What do *you* deliver that justifies your debut? Moreover, why must people stick around for future product launches when they've already sampled what you have to offer?

Growth *must* be the answer. A steel base doesn't make a skyscraper; you must keep assembling the trusses, reinforcing the material to construct a dazzling structure. And even once it's on sturdy legs, you can't let the building wither away to the elements. Maintenance must be upheld.

If you look at the tallest structures in New York City, they don't just undergo rigorous regulations to ensure they can carry massive weights for the traffic they allow. The owners constantly introduce new amenities to attract visitors. Skyscrapers demand a level of craftsmanship that'll magnetize hundreds of people off novelty alone; yet still, a slew of curious glances can't pay off the gargantuan costs forever. You'll need to keep a consistent flow of traffic, whether that be renting out office spaces, providing food, spectacles, amusement and so on. People tire of the same offerings, and need to shift overtime, which is why you saw a lot of the office-oriented buildings switch management during the pandemic. They couldn't serve their market under the constrained conditions, but the strategies they had in place were targeted towards a specific need that wasn't relevant any longer. Certainly, the leaders they had on board were prepped for a narrow set of challenges; thus, many companies failed to adapt and had to switch hands with a better-equipped buyer.

You don't want to be the business that collapses during a storm. It's essential that you adapt to volatility; understandably, that might sound like an oxymoron, because can something be truly unpredictable if there is a way to anticipate it?

The answer is yes. You can't predict a storm far into the future (unless you're clairvoyant, or secretly moonlighting as a genius weatherman), but you can assemble a structure that is toughened against the worst of disasters. That's what we call building durability. Any successful business will need to be robust, so succession planning entwines as a means of ensuring that security.

Importance is Often Overlooked or Underplayed

People don't talk about problems enough. This goes for every aspect of life. We're stuck in a toxic positivity cycle that slowly dismantles institutions from the inside out. People don't respond well to criticism, and that trickles down to their performance in the workplace. Weaknesses are interpreted as a reflection of their character. "But if my manager says that I'm not fast enough at my job, does that mean that I wasn't as smart as I thought?" It's easy to question your capabilities when they're put under a magnifying glass, especially when feedback is somehow swept in with negativity nowadays.

No entity is above criticism. By nature, as a business, you're exposing yourself to the broadest amount of exposure possible.

Inevitably, that means you'll resonate with a selection of consumers, while spurning others. A brand that is beloved by everyone and for every launch is one that stands for nothing; essentially, a business that is doomed to drown in its blandness. You must make a statement, no matter how unconventional it is, as that's what will win loyalty with customers.

Simultaneously, you must note that the people who propagate your mission at the beginning aren't exactly the people who'll be compatible with it at later stages. Even if you're not the most polarizing brand in the marketplace, there will be moments when you must reevaluate your internal performance. Certain mindsets that worked when you were a 15-people team won't perfectly translate to a multinational franchise. You *have to* look inwards and hone your leadership, but that'll only occur if you identify the importance. A lot of businesses, sadly, don't recognize that their management is dragging them down. Either that, or they refuse to let go of what's silently positioning them.

If you're a company member that works outside of the C-suite, you might feel vindicated to hear that your managers are just as responsible for measuring their success as they are yours. Think of it as, when you're at the top of the mountain, you're no longer going to meet other climbers to tell you where to step or where to go next. You've reached the peak, but that doesn't mean you're at safety. Safety is at the ground level, where there are no immediate threats to your position. There are countless factors that can endanger you while you're reposing on the top of a mountain. A sudden avalanche, terrain caving in, oxygen depletion, even wild animals depending on the elevation. Hopefully, the industry you serve doesn't require that you tiptoe around equal health concerns, although it is likely that you "flourishing" on the top can be snatched away as quickly as it was granted. That's the reason you're consulting this book, no?

When the terrain changes, and the leaders' scope gradually narrows, it is imperative that they take on new perspectives to sustain — not to mention strengthen — their reach. Succession planning is the preparations you take to train the next generation of managers. It is the preparations you take to ensure that all potential gaps in your organization are closed, so that when operations falter, you can count on a strong foundation to carry you through the hardship.

$$\textit{Cost to Train} = \frac{\textit{Total Training Costs}}{\textit{Total Number of Employees Trained}}$$

*Where **Total Training Costs** Includes:*

- Training Materials & Resources
- Training Fees, Internal or External
- Venue Costs, if Applicable
- Employee Time Spent in Training, Calculated as Opportunity Cost
- Travel Expenses Related to Training, if Applicable

If more C-suite executives viewed management as a revolving trial, they'd proactively seek new leadership and center the development of others outside of themselves. Now, this isn't to say that these professionals are narrowly focused on themselves, because it is normal for any professional to relate to the struggles of those in their realm. Even if you work under the same roof as others (which, technically, C-suite executives in large companies tend to occupy the highest floor, so perhaps this is a loose analogy), your day-to-day responsibilities will greatly differ depending on the role you take. C-suite executives oversee a lot of people who, under the right training, can potentially rival their authority. It seems glum to note, but nothing lasts forever, and even lower-level supervisors must keep a lookout for how they compare to fresher talent.

No one wants to hear that their voice is dwindling in the workplace, but sometimes you need to invest in the strengths of others to see your own importance flourish. When it comes down to evaluations, a C-suite executive that stands behind the company's most profitable quarters will fare better than one who gripped the strictest control, to dismal returns. The corporate world can trick us into seeing the improvement of our colleagues as a negative when we must be going out of our way to teach them. Not only is it fulfilling from a human perspective (studies show that supporting others raises levels of dopamine), but it also is rational from a business perspective. A well-managed business will consider the contributions of members who "glue" the workforce together when it is performing well. It's the reason why productive employees that struggle in collaboration lose out on leadership positions; you want to reward the people who surpass their peers' output, but if their performance drives others' down, then why would you place them in a position of increased power?

This traces back to our point about "toxic positivity." C-suite executives owe it to themselves, and their responsibilities, to reflect on what blind spots they may have left to fester so that they can seek professionals who'd compensate for those vulnerabilities. Problems only aggravate overtime. The longer you pretend as if your current team can operate at the efficiency it has forever, the higher the chance its flaws will explode in your face in an irreversible way in the long run. I'd imagine the office owners who didn't diversify their investments prior to the decade are now regretting having not picked up younger perspectives.

Or they blissfully vacationed to the Caymans on the fat stacks of stock payouts they earned up until then. Who knows if they delighted in having not mentored younger talent, knowing that it'd mean more resources to share?

For the sake of this argument, we'll choose to believe that they did cry a little over the lost earning potential.

Gatekeeping Costs Performance

Ask about anyone trying to climb up in the corporate world, and they'll say that they're repulsed by gatekeeping. It's human nature to react negatively to exclusion that affects us, but when the tables turn, many choose to ignore the issue.

When you take the time to deliberate it, gatekeeping can be a strategy for those in power. They don't have to fear their positions being taken by a more qualified candidate when they manipulate assessments — either with toxic management or neglecting to observe them in the first place.

Ageism is a huge issue in the workplace. Professionals who have spent a lot of time in the workforce experience troubles adapting to the ever-encroachment of technology. Newer workers aren't necessarily quicker learners, but their familiarity with digital devices lends them an advantage to traversing the market that their seniors lack. This drives a rift between younger and older workers, the latter of whom are commonly pitted against "faster" talents who can accomplish their responsibilities in half the time.

With the cost of living on the rise, it isn't hard to grasp why someone would want to be extra guarded about their employment. Your replacement can swoop in and disrupt your lifestyle as you know it. We expect for our authorities to lead with maturity and reject the unhealthy impulses we fall victim, but they are ultimately human like us. A short-sighted manager might ice subordinates out of career opportunities simply for the fact they wish to protect what they have.

At least, until they feel the consequences of a static company structure. When you glance at the C-suite makeup of the largest conglomerates in the world, you'll glean that their CEOs rotate on a short basis. In the past, you wouldn't flinch to see a CEO run a notorious business until they were too old to get into their office chair, but as of recently, companies are growing more and more aware of the need for evolution. That is why you are seeing pioneers who ushered industries into new eras drop from their responsibilities. Their quantity of labor didn't take a hit, per se, but its productive upsides paled in comparison to the talents seen elsewhere. If anyone realizes the value of welcoming an outside lens to a new level of an organization, it'd be the visionaries who changed the business world. Hence why large companies successfully restructure, adapt, and skim as needed.

The thing about human instincts is that although we all encounter them, the workplace isn't supposed to be a facility for overcoming your impulses. Yes, you must be taking feedback in stride and be encouraged to grow, but a lot of people mistake "accidents" as "unavoidable contingencies."

A mistake doesn't need intention to be detrimental. And intention isn't the instigator of all faults. At some point, problems point towards a pattern as a streak of poor decisions.

Gatekeeping is one example of that. If the upper management in your organization struggle to hold themselves accountable, it's no wonder the business fails to produce divergent voices in times of regression. It's not like change can be whipped out of thin air. Where were the gradual steps towards internal development?

This also raises the stain gatekeeping leaves on subordinates. Your workers are a lot like sponges in the sense they'll look to authority for what behaviors must and mustn't be rewarded. When they witness powerful figures taking home large bonuses for middling work, then they'll assume that they, too, can thrive while underperforming. If the business really cared about productivity, they'd be on the lookout for talents who do challenge themselves on the clock. But too many business leaders turn a blind eye to assets that earned their recognition, assuming they must be doing a good job because they proved themselves, however long ago. To the contrary, someone can cozy up to your personality or play a part in the best business season you've ever seen, all while regressing the longer you keep them in an invulnerable role.

Even intellectual property suffers at the hands of nonexistent succession planning. Let's look at this case study:

Maternity Leave in an Unprepared Business

An indie record label has had to see its A&R off because she's requested sudden maternity leave. Martha is a well-networked professional who was explicitly taken on the team for her connections and availability. Clients love her commitment to helping them out, even when she is out of the studio.

Due to the stigma surrounding maternity leave, Martha hesitated to disclose her pregnancy when she was interviewed for the role. Because the label operates on a tight budget (as they're independent), Martha's absence presents a series of challenges. Of course, they wish her well as she is a valuable asset to their team and would love for her to return when she feels ready. Nonetheless, the transition to seeking a fill-in professional is strenuous. Large corporations have no issue offloading additional work on employees when a labor shortage occurs. If the increased responsibilities prompt people to quit, they have a broad enough skill pool to extract from.

Alas, the indie label differentiates itself from bigger competitors for its intimate size, flaunting a small labor capacity allows them to not only interact closely with clients but also save on costs. This is a strong USP when the market responds well, but if there is one consistent truth about the business world, it is that your field is dynamic. If it's not a random competitor that's disrupting sales, then internal conflicts will strike you at random. No one is particularly predisposed to problems, but modest entities can't afford to undertake massive trials. Losing the sole "talent" in an important role can fragment the fabric of a company.

Prior to Martha's leave, the label begins processing candidates to replace her position. They hire a new A&R, Jonathan. Jonathan integrates into the company culture fairly quickly. He has experience in the field, so this isn't his first time recruiting artists and negotiating contracts. What does surprise him, however, is the lack of organization that is slowly creeping onto his table.

You see, Martha holds a wealth of files and contacts that aren't accessible as she's departed the building. This means that they must reach her for every single need: ask for this client's number, call up this person, and so on. As a newcomer, Jonathan is quickly frustrated by the amount of back-and-forth he has been dragged into. His managers brush it off, arguing the snug nature of the company necessitates close communication. They only start to absorb the effects of it as Martha wearies from being haggled during her break and corresponds at a sparser rate. Jonathan, despite showing promise during the screening process, flounders at his position because there is no transitional material available for him to learn Martha's knowledge.

This is just one case study that exemplifies the burden of poor succession planning. You may be inclined to counter, "but Jonathan is a new hire, of course he'll be unfamiliar with the ropes!" but within a small or mid-sized company, would similar circumstances reflect differently if they promoted internally?

A lot of companies don't have targeted procedures in place. Their leaders ignorantly assume that everything will operate when it must, as it must, so the trusty employee that lifts the rest of their underperforming team won't just spontaneously stop showing up to work, or their star manager won't have to request maternity leave. It's easy to dismiss the future as an unreachable enigma that'll affect you when it does, but the reality is that those who inadequately prepare are the ones who resign first.

Maturity stems from acknowledging that you must encapsulate the worst-case possibilities, even when it feels like you're on Cloud Nine. Carving out the dream team doesn't mean you're free to let results flow as they arise; if anything, it marks the inception of your next stage. *Preservation.*

Take it like this — if you've bought a coffee maker that brews your morning joe just as you like it, you'd hate for the machine to break down, leaving you with subpar tools to rely on, right?

It can be costly to buy reinforcements for the same asset. You probably can't name a single person who has bought the same espresso maker twice, but I can imagine that everyone you know has the basic appliances to make coffee at home should their machine fail. It's basic provisions. If a fuse blows out, or an electricity surge destroys the wiring, how are you going to adapt your routine? Unless you want to slug along to work because you missed out on your daily preparations, then it is logical that you have a backup in store in case of emergencies.

In this sense, succession planning acts as a failsafe which, in the event of a disaster, is crucial for preventing severe damage. C-suite executives must be aligned with moves that'll ensure the company's long-term success, thus driving the need for development procedures.

Loss of Continuity of Service

As a company expands, its internal culture will noticeably shift. Hopefully for the better, considering you'll want to see improvements as you service a broader market; not only must operations raise productive output, but management must be drafting broader strategies.

With a surplus of responsibilities added to your plate, it's easy for things to get jumbled up. Suddenly, the HR team on Floor 2 are corresponding with a dedicated tech team on the ground floor, when you're accustomed to contracting professionals for specific causes. When you can not only muster the expenses of more professionals but need to stretch your workforce to meet market demand, the pace at which you need to train accelerates. We aren't just looking at the onboarding PowerPoints that you've been recycling. With more professionals added to the lower rungs of your organization, there needs to be sufficient leadership to guide them in assimilating into the culture. See it like how a classroom must follow the perfect student to teacher ratio for the pupils to get the most out of their lessons. Employees also need access to the right proportion of authority to thrive, otherwise the company will become a disoriented mess.

During the formative years of a business' existence, it's generally easier to prime new leaders as the workforce is so closely interconnected that passing down information is akin to walking to the next room. You can email your supervisor and expect a reply the next day, perhaps even call up the CEO and get a response because operations aren't that massive.

However, the scale of operations fragments what we take advantage of. Comfort is the enemy of success, but it'd be dishonest to claim we all haven't grown attached to a luxury that was soon wrested away. It's natural to indulge in nice things, but it's not rational to blind yourself to the fact that they are rare privileges. Especially as a C-suite executive, you must be molding your strategy around the fact that at some point in the future, the market will receive your offerings harshly. It might be because your in-house skillset doesn't meet their expectations any longer, might also be because the market is undergoing a dramatic shift. Whatever the case, you don't want to fumble everything you've worked up towards over a rough period. You'll want the chance to learn from any mistakes you made and fortify the business for the future. That's why it is so important to adapt not only the skillset you hire as the company expands, but also be vigilant about the leadership procedures it holds. Has the honing process been updated recently? What's the update on its impacts in the last month? Year?

To draw a connection with another section in this book, internal evaluations must not be limited to a singular timeframe in a year. Assessments must be revolving and tangible. In other words, employees must see the results of their peers being observed, and see the steps being taken to elect future leaders. If those processes stagger, mayhem will ensue when the company broaches a period where management ebbs in reach.

Gaps in Processes and Procedures Cause Turnover

It's easy to talk about what we would do if we were fortunate. "I'd donate to the poor. I'd buy houses for my friends and families. I'd start the biggest business known to man."

If everyone had a heap of fortune fall on their lap, they swear they'd be millionaires. But if everyone were lucky, then luck would be a paradox — wouldn't luxuries just be the norm, then?

So, we chase and reinvent new sorts of ideals. A lot of them pivoted on the belief that under the right conditions, we'd be a thousand times more successful than we already are. And that's some wishful thinking to apply in your regular life, when bills pile up and commitments fall through over empty promises. But when you have others dependent on you for their financial livelihoods?

Yeah, the "future" doesn't cut it.

Your employees can't wait around for adequacy. Just as there are dozens of talents you've sifted through to land on a selection of hires, there are thousands of IPs emerging in the market every single day; you're not especially for providing a job. Especially if that job presents more stress than it does benefits.

If you glance at the studies emerging on shifts in the workforce, you'll see that younger professionals are choosing workplaces where mental health upsides precede other offerings. The new crop of talents isn't putting up with domineering bosses. Even in the past, you could only last so long without vetting your authorities, but as the seams continue to burst within toxic organizational cultures, C-suite professionals must validate that they aren't contributing to the problem.

Unless you want to suffer the burden of turnover.

Turnover is associated with high-stress environments. Fast-food restaurants bleed hires quicker than anyone, if not ironic considering their speed of service, while corporations tend to retain senior employees for months at minimum.

Despite the varying demands between these two types of environments, one truth persists; when you have hasty leadership, they won't be able to foster a lasting work culture.

It doesn't take a huge amount of calculation for a professional to gauge whether a business is operating efficiently. If they sign up for the job anticipating a specific set of responsibilities, and instead being offloaded with a ton of demands that weren't communicated during the interview process, they have reason to complain. If those complaints aren't heeded, they're going to quit. You've quite literally lured them into a job where they're being underpaid for their labor. A faulty leadership system is bound to ward skilled people off as they detect that there's something wrong with your organization. If they do have the threshold to stick around, don't think that it's because the others weren't "perseverant" enough to keep up with your standards. I'd wager a guess that they're only present because messy performance means messy evaluations, making it much easier to slack on the job than it would if you had proper management. There's a reason dishonesty surges in unstable communities. When the people elected to look after them aren't distributing the right resources, then they'll achieve it through underhanded methods.

The Hire In-House Dilemma

Everyone is tense for the moment. Corporate has been eying a new authority. The boots on the ground have predicted it and are awaiting the decision.

Within their team, there's a standout worker who has been an asset during trying times. Their peers look to them as a quasi-leader, so if they got promoted, it'd be like more of the same. This person has already proven themselves to hold leadership qualities; a promotion would only be a matter of officially recognizing that.

The process goes through, and it turns out the latest pick is not an in-house promotion, but rather a hire from outside. HR explored the skills person network to identify someone best fit for the job. The person is kind, knowledgeable, and friendly, but some employees can't help the bitter feelings towards them. This feels like an act of betrayal. Corporate constantly talks about how the organization is a big family, so why did they neglect the candidate that was right beneath their nose?

In case you haven't caught the dramatics, this is a highly exaggerated example of what can occur within companies. The time for succession approaches, and employees are at the edge of their seats wondering who'll be bossing them around for the remainder of their time there. Will it be Kaylee, who is never not pedantic about policies? Will it be Kyle, who puts colleagues at ease with his laid-back approach?

Leadership shifts are some of the most impactful moves a company can make. As they affect the company's operations, their outcomes are felt inside and outside of the companies.

Consumers will absorb the positives of their broadened power, if that is the case, while employees will experience the day-to-day consequences of switched hands.

People are normally resistant to change. Even if you relieve employees of the supervisor who'd been calling out for years, they'll face an initial, bumpy period adapting to their diligent successor. You can't reform the way people spend most of their day and expect that they immediately adjust to a new set of standards.

With that in mind, it is essential that C-suite executives understand that employees are not your friends. This must be non-intuitive, and certainly not interpreted as heartless. If there is any mentality that demonstrates a lack of care, it would be subjecting the people who drive your profits to a mismanaged environment. Don't your employees deserve a leader who'll guide them towards the highest amount of effort with the littlest amount of effort? They must be encouraged to be productive with their labor, not strain themselves for the sake of a shortsighted decision; yes, you may ruffle some feathers by considering candidates from a broad pool, but the temporary backlash pales compared to the benefits. In the long term, you'll be thanking yourself for empowering the talent who knows how to handle a team.

Of course, life is at its best when it's balanced, so don't forget to consider those under your wing as well. It's all about broadening your lens to make the best decisions. Even you in the C-suite can miss certain areas at your elevation. Don't be shy to seek out direct feedback to learn the standouts within each department and remember to keep consistent evaluations so that your assessments don't paint an inaccurate depiction.

Cost of Succession Planning

At this point in the book, you've likely identified an underlying pattern: every strategy that is for the better of the business takes a lot to implement. And we're not just speaking in hypothetical "willpower" or some other variation of motivational speaker, but the exhaustion of tangible resources.

Living up to the saying that nothing good comes without sacrifice, the value of succession planning cannot be reaped without cinching your resources to some degree. You'll have to rearrange how you distribute your budget, lest you splurge too much on onboarding and too little on the processes for priming leadership.

Procedures don't create themselves. You'll have to dedicate someone towards devising the plan, and while you oversee the most responsibility in the company, you're not omnipotent. Your performance depends on offloading work when it is in the best interest of productivity to do so, so middle management will have to craft the strategies.

As your subordinates soak up the burden of propelling this mission, they'll lose valuable time on their regular responsibilities. If this severely impacts their performance in the workplace, you'll have to take in more help to maintain the same level of productivity. Not to mention, you'll need to approve any major processes they seek to implement.

You can see how the costs quickly add up. It's not as if you just throw a bunch of money and encouragement at a cause, then expect it to flourish overnight. Development takes time, and as with all areas of a business, you'll have to invest a significant amount to observe changes.

A lot of businesses purposely skirt around this obligation because they don't want to muster the expenses. Think of it like this: the life cycle for an employee can be short, whether they're at the top of the ladder or one of the boots on the ground. Why not ride the wave for as long as you can, leaving your successors to bear the fallout of your negligence when it's time?

It's a destructive, selfish mentality to hold, but a lot of people act in their best interest — even more so in an environment that is sculpted to propagate competition. You can't assume that the C-suite executives that rose before you passed the reins with optimistic intentions, because a lot of people only abandon ship once it's sinking.

That is why it is so important you utilize your position of power effectively. Proactive maneuvers can offset the costs of positive habits in the long run, but only if you're ready to sacrifice certain comforts at the start.

Time isn't the only currency on par with dollars; the trust you can lose with employees is worth just as much, if not more than the resources you're forced to expend. Once you tarnish your workers' faith in your company's operations, it'll take a lot of time and consistent ethics to restore your reputation. And this doesn't go for solely internal perspectives. Inevitably, your target market will feel the effects of a disorganized leadership structure. If you're lucky, you'll miraculously avert the impacts of not preparing for a sudden death or illness amongst your management. But for most entities, it is better for both the authorities and subordinates to know that there are safeguards ready in the event of unforeseen changes.

Real-World Connection

The president of a software company has opted for retirement. Their subordinates send them off with warm emotions, having appreciated their contributions for the duration of their leadership. The average employee isn't closely acquainted with the inner workings of the C-suite, so they don't fret over who's lined up for the dazzling position. Maybe it'll be a longtime manager, or maybe they'll extend their search outside of the company. Regardless, they'll get to form their opinions when the new management style is observed.

Meanwhile, the two VPs are in the running for the empty position. Their compatibility is a no-brainer as they're soaked in the company's culture, are intimate with the President's methods and areas of weakness and are familiar to various members of the company. It's a far more seamless succession than it would be if they sought talent elsewhere, and for a position as empowered as a president's, you want to err on the cautious side.

Thus, you yield a pair of two qualified candidates for a role one person can assume.

...and, that role happens to hold ultimate authority in the organization, so there's no one above to enforce the succession. The nominees will have to decide the best fit among themselves, and you can bet they didn't work their way up the corporate ladder with feeble personalities. A president's role is a once-in-a-lifetime opportunity, especially when you've been loyal to a company for several years.

Tensions stir. Both VPs think that they're the better choice for the succession, and since no one will quietly step to the side, it rages on longer than is productive for the company. The problem with successions is that they must be thorough, and vigilance requires a certain amount of time. Yet, there is a cutoff when the length of time you'd dedicate towards making a single decision or move isn't worth the outcome it'd drive. Even under the best of circumstances, you can't have people, let alone the most powerful people in your company, lingering on one issue for eternity.

At this point, the battle has trickled down to the VP's subordinates. The employees can feel the bitterness of the succession war, and it significantly dampers their impression of the VP's capabilities. When one of the two do get elected, they would've exposed a side of them that is less than mature to the public. Authorities are supposed to lead by behavior, setting examples beyond the policies they preach. It isn't auspicious when the person you depend on for your livelihood is fighting over something that must've been decided at some point in the previous president's reign. They must've had a plan in place before they waned off from their responsibilities.

Opportunities

Illustrate a Roadmap

Hands-off instruction is a lot easier than a lot of people take them to be. As a C-suite executive, you inadvertently occupy the position of a teacher through the rules you pass down and the excellence you model; every teacher must know the value of a streamlined lesson plan, which ties into succession planning.

Executing a strategy involves mingling different approaches, many of which serve as tests, many of which flourish as eventual successes. One method that has stood the test of time is visual instruction.

Exposure is a powerful tool. You confront someone with a particular idea enough, and it will seep into their subconscious. This is why psychologists emphasize the importance of positive reinforcement; if you're surrounded by an environment that is full of toxicity and negative language, then you'll go on to embody those traits before you even realize it's transferred onto you. Ever made a new friend and caught yourself picking up their unique quirks? The people we talk to casually inform our language and mannerisms; it's no wonder that our workplaces, where we often spend the bulk of our waking hours, can morph our performance. You can be the best employee in the world, and all it takes is coping with the wrong job for too long for your qualities to deteriorate.

The good thing about development is that it's almost always possible to change a tailored environment. A workplace, while susceptible to the volatility of the marketplace, isn't quite so varied as the outside world. At least if you're running your business properly, your HR isn't advised to take on any talent that shows up at your door. There's a narrow pool of workers you invite within your walls, and those are likely to share personality traits. That makes the process of influencing them easier. You'll be able to observe the effectiveness of your strategies swiftly because if it fails with one department, the likelihood it will resonate with another is slim.

Returning to the focal point, roadmaps are a robust strategy for spotlighting growth opportunities in a company. If you're maintaining the career section on your company website properly, there must be a thorough look at what there is to attain if you seek different roles. But many businesses don't even have a functional URL in place, not to speak of a presentable roadmap.

You must see employee education as an investment. If you show your assets a reason to expand in value, they will take the strides to improve their career situation. But if you're dodgy about whether promotions are even available to those who remain loyal to the company (so many businesses rely on nepotism, so it isn't far-fetched to assume that they'll promote on favoritism), then you'll give reason for employees to prime themselves for opportunities elsewhere.

Employees and their leaders are bound to relationships like many other facets of life. And a common trend in relationships is for one party to expect more out of others than they do for themselves. If you don't lend the impression that you care for your employments' growth to any degree, then why must they strain themselves trying to figure out what'll awe you under your nebulous expectations? It's more sensible to switch to an employer that has clear barometers in place, an employee who exhibits "x" performance will reap "y" returns, and so on. C-suite executives who fail to outline these possibilities won't bolster a ton of morale amongst their employees.

Not only do roadmaps communicate that you care about professional development, but it also clarifies what employees must do to reach their desired positions. It may surprise you, but climbing from one position to another isn't as clear-cut as it may appear to you as it is to new hires in the corporate world. For starters, there are a lot of industry-specific rules that prevent professionals from transferring skills from one role to another. This forces them to seek experience through indirect steps that lead them towards qualification, but they'll only embark on the correct trajectory if they know where to go. So many company resources can be unnecessarily depleted if someone is occupying the wrong role, especially if they'd be better off in another position.

Feeder groups are the intermediary between novices and higher-ranking, specialized roles; they can serve as a useful training ground to hone professionals prior to their transfer, but only if they are advertised correctly. Have resources spread around that educate workers on the different opportunities available, as well as what the roadmap looks like for promotions up each pathway.

Roadmaps Differentiate Who is Prepared Versus Who Relies on Experience as a Crutch

Time is the essence of habit, but performance isn't a 1:1 reflection of the experience you have at a company. As established in previous sections, a talent can swoop into your business at any time, outdoing those who preceded them. There are countless employees who've remained at the same company for years yet have displayed little growth compared to those who came after them. This isn't a slight on their character; some people are faster learners, plus, not everyone is so ambitious to pursue a higher ranking. You're going to encounter personalities who are fine with taking on the same instructions until they retire from work. That is okay, if you recognize the bounds of what they fulfill in the organization.

As we discuss how roadmaps clarify the steps to qualify for a specific promotion, it is essential that we educate employees on the qualities that make a fitting leader. The best worker in your tech department can be the weakest manager. Just because someone excels in one aspect doesn't mean that their promise will translate elsewhere. Some operations are best left churning to their own rhythm, and that includes the particularities surrounding authority. Maybe you have a candidate for a planned succession who has been loyal to the company for long but has yet to show that they're capable of guiding a team. It's easy to think you'll kill two birds with one stone by throwing them a promotion, but will that really be a reward in the long run? I don't imagine they'll thank you for drowning under the weight of excess responsibility. Also, if their broadened powers are that detrimental, then they'll compromise the security of their job in the process. They'll have essentially gotten a taste of what it's like to work at a higher rank before being chucked all the way to the bottom.

If you ask me, that doesn't sound very reward-worthy.

Each Role must Bring New Experiences and Knowledge

If we view the workplace as a continuous track for growth, it seems inevitable that roles must be molded to develop employees.

To be more specific, the facilities, the tasks workers interact with must be aligned with their skillful growth. There are a lot of positions that are erroneously dismissed as "filler" or "easy" titles. If someone is showing up to provide labor, their work must never be misconstrued as anything but that. It is one thing to differentiate professionals' reach within a company based on their rank, and a whole other to underscore the value of their contributions.

At the same time, we must question the expectations of the establishment they serve if their offerings are not clear. Is the system pushing workers to develop on the job? If someone is cycling through the same task for a decade, then they'll only get better at that specific task. Even then, it's hard to improve at a singular focus after you've reached a certain point. You'd have to actively exert yourself to beat a certain pace or productive capacity, and how many employees go out of their way to do more than they're expected to?

As the professional with the most oversight in the organization, you must be venturing out to educate employees on how they can absorb new lessons and experiences. Try setting up initiatives that are accessible to different departments (if applicable to your company structure) or invite speakers that are versed in subjects unfamiliar to your targeted employees. They can broaden the scope of their knowledge by listening to the viewpoint outside of their usual circle.

Assign Resources and Expectations in the Beginning

Remember what we talked about on proactivity? When you put a system in motion to account for certain results in the future, then you can guarantee that you'll yield success in the long term.

Succession planning lives up to its name: to succeed at the endeavor, you mustn't shuffle last minute to throw together a strategy that'll change the company structure.

Hasty efforts produce hasty results. And don't trust that those quick instances of feedback will always be positive. No one can predict every single obstacle they'll have to prepare for at the onset of their business journey, but when you practice vigilance, proactivity must happen as a byproduct.

If you're just learning about the importance of succession planning from this book, don't fear that it is too late. Even if you've already suffered as a result of a rushed authority handover, you can benefit from learning how you'll avoid a repetition in the future. You can't rewind the hands of a clock to return to the past, but you can plan to limit future mistakes.

Check whether there are accessible resources for employees to know what opportunities you have. Are they posted up in bulletins at the front of the office? Are they dispersed through cubicles when they clock in, or are they mass-distributed through email?

You aren't gathering the entire company every workday, so you must take advantage of the indirect networks you have at your disposal to reach them. Written information, digital knowledge, and visual demonstrations all support the goal of spreading knowledge. It can be as simple as drafting a career tree from one job, then extending to another, and then another. Soon, you'll have covered the whole organization.

Addressing this early on helps to create movers and shakers, rather than people happy with just a 9-5. When you go the extra mile to bolster the experience in the workplace, your subordinates will feel the effects of that resolve. Any ambitious talent will be inspired to join the ranks of a leadership that is driven to lift them up.

Develop the Organization so That You're More Than an Organization Chart

Employees need to see the moving blocks in action to grasp that these processes are fluid, rather than performative. There must be observable impacts of your planning. While it's nice to operate in silence without outside interference, a company cannot thrive when it's strung together by isolated parts. There must be a continuous flow of feedback that is shaping the approaches, the people involved and where they're pulled towards.

For example, one set of employees might train their sights on a position in HR. Perhaps they double majored in that program or gained experience there on the side. The standard route to attain that role is through seeking positions in the company that'll align them with relevant roles. HR's existing team will take notice of their potential and want to vouch for a professional that'll be a positive asset to their department.

Somewhere along the line, there will be employees who discover this is, in fact, not their natural calling. There can be a multitude of reasons why someone chooses to diverge onto a different path; and no matter what it may be, you owe a supportive system to your employees that'll allow them to transition seamlessly if they want to aggressively pursue a different trajectory.

This does not mean that you need to lavish all the resources in the world on any individual who proclaims that they'd like to take a step up in the organization. As with every aspect of C-suite management, you must exercise discernment while overseeing your succession procedures. Ensure that there are resources and facilities available for those who want to grow into new titles, but don't spend everything your brand is worth on a narrow, fixed goal.

Succession is Ongoing

No matter how old a company is, businesses will always be able to outlast their living components — sounds grim, and I don't mean to make a *Terminator* or other dystopian sci-fi reference, but you must recognize that your skilled assets are ephemeral. No one can guarantee that a brand will forever stand the test of time, but if you look at the most iconic corporations in human history, you'll notice one overarching fact: none of their founders are present as CEOs.

For some of the fresher industry disruptors, this won't equate to the founders being gone forever. Maybe they simply retired or decided to distance themselves from the stress of a round-the-clock job. One thing that's assured is they'll need new replacements. The managers who respond to them will need new reinforcements to ease their responsibilities as the business expands. People are always moving within a company; if the employees in your company are entirely content with remaining where they are, then there is something wrong with the career education that is being provided. Either that, or you're facing such a high turnover that nobody sees themselves sticking around so long that they'll need a sized load of responsibilities.

Move People from the Bottom Up

Promotions can feel like a prickly subject to broach in general. If you let in someone into a "prized" position from the outside, then you risk being interpreted by your employees as disloyal. If you exclusively pick from an insular group, then your workforce will take it as a sign that they never stood a chance if they didn't possess the right characteristics.

As we've discussed earlier in this section, balance is the mediator of all issues in life. There are ways to navigate sensitive situations without producing the most amount of fallout, and there are also strategies you can follow to not bristle so many of your subordinates when you plan successions.

For starters, you must address your internal biases when you assign promotions. As a C-suite executive, you occupy an elevation in a company that few people have access to. The day-to-day outlook for boots on the ground is easier to imagine for a member of middle management because they've likely experienced those responsibilities, but how many people can say that they know what it's like to be a CFO? What about a VP?

There's no harm in maintaining exclusivity within areas that require high quality-control. You can't just have anyone ambush a healthcare role, for example, that demands a ton of expertise and diligence. A senior surgeon must carry the right certifications and recommendations to be trusted with the lives of vulnerable patients. The average business isn't, thankfully, handling fragile lives when they contemplate management shake ups, but they are fiddling with a fabric that can be easily torn.

Keep an eye out for whether the most powerful members in your company are considering people based on their match for a role foremost, or their proximity. Are people being lifted from the bottom up, or are chances in the favor of those who already had the right fortune to succeed? It isn't motivating to see the same crop of people get rewarded repeatedly. Worse, extracting from the same pool limits perspectives. A flourishing business will need insights from diverse views, so you want to welcome fresh talents as much as you do for employees that have been loyal to the business the longest.

Mentoring Programs

After touching upon the value of hands-off approaches, it appears timely that we appreciate hands-on instruction as well. In school, many of us learn about distinct divisions of learners — one visual, another olfactory, and the other tactile. Recent research has suggested that these categories are arbitrary, and a strong learning strategy will serve any student regardless of where their preferences (supposedly) lie.

When we look at the data, it makes sense that science changed their conclusions, as validating as it was to cling to these "special" categories. A person can enjoy reading but become overwhelmed by getting drowned in textbook review. A person can ace every test with a specific lecturer while struggling to follow the instruction of a different teacher.

Plus, you wouldn't trust a surgeon to perform an operation because they memorized a medical textbook. You must gain hands-on experience to be honed for your job's responsibilities. Many companies make the mistake of assuming their employees will learn through their own roles and resources, but that is an indirect form of learning. They'll need an actual trial on the training ground to learn not only what they're signing up for, but if they really want to invite that to their plate in the first place.

There are people who spontaneously audition for competitions, ace the preliminary rounds, but falter when they learn of what is demanded afterwards. Not everyone wants to subject themselves to increased rigor, and it's natural for perceptions to shift when we're closely exposed to an unfamiliar ideal.

Always Develop, Plan, and Learn

Your strategy must be adaptive and consistent. Uphold your management to maintain the procedures and processes that supply this need.

Don't Be Stingy and Be Transparent.

Try to keep yourself from compartmentalizing and assess your organization from a holistic viewpoint. When you have a good judgement of the resources your company has at its disposal, as well as the talents that can be extended into different roles and levels of power, you can offset the costs of hiring temps to fill in for internals who need time off. Do note that the success of this relies on you training multiple members to know the inner workings of multiple roles. That way, one employee's absence doesn't mean that the entire department collapses; you can produce the same output even when they're away.

Avoid Fractional Positions

Hiring and outsourcing work is expensive. When you haven't properly structured your organization to operate as efficiently as possible, you won't be able to avoid that — hence why you must educate your workforce so that workers aren't clinging to roles that could be absorbed by a full-time position. If someone has such a narrow focus that their responsibility could be squeezed into another role, then it is costing dollars.

KEY TAKEAWAYS

Efficient resource management is the root of a business's success. You want to implement procedures and processes to plan the successions in your workforce so that it is equipped for growth and operates at an efficiency that curbs costs.

Author Bio

Yara Banks, MBA, CHRMAP

Contact Yara & BNX at:

BNX Financial Solutions, LLC
DBA BNX Business Advisors
Direct Line: (904)345-0070
Email: YaraB@BNXBA.com
Website: www.BNXBA.com
FL Certified WOBE and MOBE

BNX HR Planning Resource

Yara Banks is a visionary leader, HR strategist, and acclaimed author of *The Executive Blindspot: How Misalignment with HR Impacts Your Bottom Line*. With over 25 years of combined experience in HR, operations, and leadership development, Yara has earned a reputation as a trusted advisor to C-suite executives across industries. As the CEO of BNX Business Advisors, she specializes in helping organizations align their human resources strategies with overarching business goals, transforming HR into a measurable driver of growth, profitability, and innovation.

A certified Woman and Minority-Owned Business leader, Yara has worked with Fortune 500 companies, government agencies, and small businesses, offering insights that bridge the gap between leadership vision and workforce execution. Her expertise, combined with a passion for empowering businesses, has made her a sought-after keynote speaker and thought leader on organizational success.

Business Introduction

BNX Business Advisors

BNX Business Advisors is a dynamic HR consulting firm dedicated to helping organizations unlock the full potential of their human capital. Under the leadership of Yara Banks, MBA, CHRMAP, BNX takes a results-driven approach to align HR strategies with business objectives, delivering solutions that enhance productivity, reduce compliance risks, and foster a thriving workplace culture. From leadership development and post-merger integration to compliance management and organizational design, BNX serves as a strategic partner for businesses looking to grow and thrive in a competitive landscape.

Service Introduction

Empowering Leaders, Transforming Organizations

At BNX Business Advisors, we know that the true power of any organization lies in its people. Our services are designed to bridge the gap between HR and business strategy, empowering executives to make decisions that positively impact their bottom line. Key services include:

- **Leadership Development Programs**: Tailored workshops and coaching to build resilient, future-ready leaders.
- **Compliance and Risk Management**: Proactive solutions to minimize risks and meet regulatory standards.

- **Organizational Design and Post-Merger Integration**: Expert guidance to ensure seamless transitions and cultural alignment.
- **Strategic Workforce Planning**: Aligning talent strategies with long-term business objectives.

Whether you're navigating rapid growth, addressing compliance challenges, or building a high-performing team, BNX delivers solutions that drive measurable results.

Layers of Engagement

Yara Banks offers multiple ways for organizations and leaders to engage with her expertise:

1. **The Executive Blindspot Keynote Speaking**
   - **Format**: Inspirational and actionable presentations tailored for executive audiences.
   - **Focus Topics**:
     - Aligning HR with business strategy.
     - Overcoming blindspots that hinder growth and profitability.
     - Building a culture of accountability and innovation.
2. **Executive Workshops and Masterclasses**
   - **Format**: Interactive sessions designed to equip leaders with tools for HR alignment and organizational success.
   - **Example Workshops**:
     - "Closing the Gap: HR Strategies for Bottom-Line Impact"
     - "Leadership Blindspots: Identifying and Overcoming Barriers to Success"

3. **Advisory and Consulting Services**
   - **Format**: One-on-one or team advisory sessions with Yara and the BNX Business Advisors team.
   - **Focus Areas**:
     - Leadership development and succession planning.
     - Post-merger integration strategies.
     - Compliance risk mitigation.
4. **Strategic Partnerships and Retainer Packages**
   - **Format**: Long-term collaborations to embed BNX expertise into your organization.
   - **Includes**:
     - Regular strategy sessions with Yara.
     - Tailored HR solutions aligned with quarterly and annual business goals.
5. **Book-Based Learning Opportunities**
   - **Format**: Workshops and discussion sessions based on *The Executive Blindspot*.
   - **Includes**:
     - Case study analyses from the book.
     - Practical exercises to address organizational blindspots.
6. **Leadership Development Training**
   - **Format**: Customizable training solutions, including Yara's Signature Series, **LeadForward©**.
   - **Focus Areas**:
     - Enhancing emotional intelligence in leadership.
     - Building future-ready, adaptable teams.
     - Driving organizational success through empowered leadership.

- **Signature Series Highlights**:
  - The **LeadForward© Program**, a structured leadership development journey designed to prepare managers and executives to lead with confidence, vision, and purpose.

BNX Levels of Engagement

Visit our website to learn more about our HR Process,

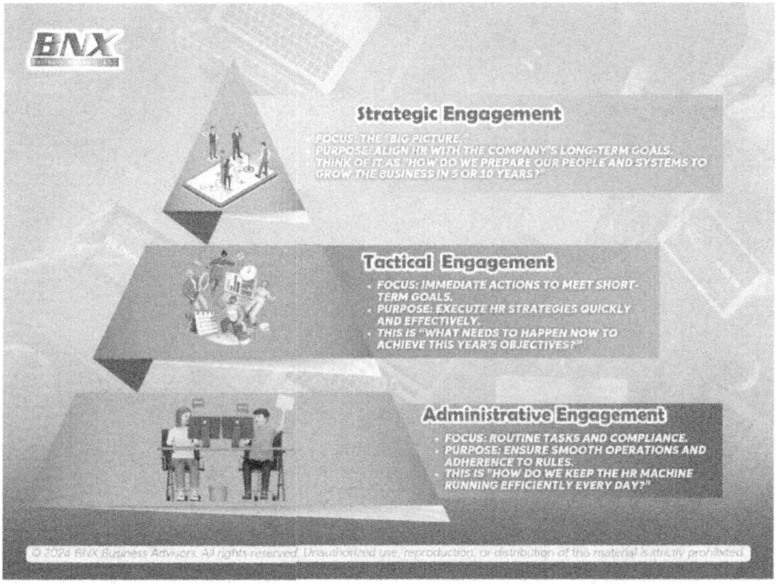

https://bnxba.com/service/human-resource-planning-development/

Made in United States
North Haven, CT
10 November 2026

22091363R00108